The Golden Girls
COOKBOOK

Cheesecakes and Cocktails!

DESSERTS AND DRINKS TO ENJOY ON THE LANAI WITH

Blanche, Rose, Dorothy, and Sophia

The Golden Girls
COOKBOOK

Cheesecakes and Cocktails!

CHRISTOPHER STYLER

FOOD PHOTOGRAPHY BY ANDREW SCRIVANI

HYPERION
AVENUE

LOS ANGELES · NEW YORK

Illustrations by Devin Taylor
Design by Amy C. King
Editorial by Adam Wilson

For information address
Hyperion Avenue,
77 West 66th Street,
New York, New York 10023.

First Hardcover Edition, September 2022
1 3 5 7 9 10 8 6 4 2
ISBN 978-1-368-07767-5
Library of Congress Control Number: 2022934203
FAC-034274-22210

Printed in the United States of America

Visit www.disneybooks.com

Contents

Dorothy

Cheesecakes

Cocktails with Dorothy

Rose

Cheesecakes

Cocktails with Rose

Blanche

Cheesecakes

Cocktails with Blanche

Sophia

Cheesecakes

Cocktails with Sophia

** Can be made with or without liquor

Introduction

PICTURE IT:
6151 Richmond Street, Miami
1985 to 1992

Inside live four women who share this home (with its fabulous lanai) in addition to sharing laughter, friendship, and an impressive amount of cheesecake.

After a rocky start as roommates (as they shared with us in "The Way We Met"), Dorothy, Blanche, and Rose bonded over their mutual love of cheesecake. From that point on, regardless of occasional friction or flat-out fights, they gathered around the kitchen table, often with Sophia acting as a kind of Sicilian Yoda. They talked, they laughed, they ate cheesecake. And it was over this delicious dessert that they discussed the day-to-day complexities of life: dating, Blanche's boyfriends, family problems, Blanche's boyfriends, tales of St. Olaf and Sicily, and Blanche's boyfriends.

A faithful fan of the *The Golden Girls* can only imagine what kind of cheesecakes they would bake if they put their minds to it. It's easy to picture Sophia topping off her Petrillo family recipe for Double Fudge Amaretto Ricotta Cheesecake (page 132) with sweetened mascarpone cream and crumbled amaretti cookies. Or Rose dolloping whipped cream onto a slice of pumpkin cheesecake (page 76). Fans

BLANCHE (looking at the box Rose is holding): What's that?

ROSE: *Oh, I'm sorry, I know it's awful, but I have this incredible sweet tooth.*

DOROTHY: What is it?

ROSE: *Cheesecake.*

BLANCHE: What kind?

ROSE: *Chocolate.*

DOROTHY: Oh, I think this could be the beginning of a beautiful friendship.

might picture Dorothy taking a methodical approach, making sure all ingredients were lined up and ready to go before she started baking her classic Brooklyn cheesecake (page 50). And Blanche? We can imagine she would act *(act?)* a little helpless in the kitchen and call on Jake from VIP Catering to come and give her a hand with her Southern-inspired cheesecake recipes.

Cocktails and other beverages were shared with equal enthusiasm on Richmond

Street. Or, in the case of Stinking Hot Toddies (page 100), a little less enthusiasm. Sometimes beverages were enjoyed after first impressions: Dr. Jonathan Newman was offered a cordial when he came over for dinner to meet Rose's roommates. (That might also have been a reward for making it through a sometimes awkward dinner!) Whether sipping lemonade on the lanai, sharing a Sloe Gin Fizz with Dorothy's lecherous physician boyfriend, or sharing in hot chocolate with little marshmallows, beverages were a part of everyday life in the Girls' home.

These recipes for cheesecakes and cocktails are offered in the spirit of festivity and as a way to celebrate *The Golden Girls* in the kitchen and on the lanai. Or, if you're in Brooklyn and find yourself without a lanai, on the fire escape. Fire up the oven, break out the cocktail shaker, and get ready to rock 'n' roll!

Cheesecakes

MAKING CRUSTS

To crust or not to crust? Some folks don't consider a cheesecake a proper cheesecake without one. Others shrug at the idea. There's no denying, however, that certain crust/cheesecake matches are made in heaven.

Picture a creamy, rich New York–style cheesecake (page 50) without its sheath of buttery graham cracker crust. Dorothy can't—it would go against everything Brooklyn she holds dear. And if you're going to head down the road to decadence with Blanche, you may as well go for broke and include the chocolate cookie crust that envelops her Mocha Chocolata Ya! Ya! Cheesecake (page 109).

All crusts can be made up to a day in advance but can also be made right when you start prepping the cheesecake batter. (Baking ahead means one less thing to do if you have a date with the hunk from the Center.) In either case, they should be baked soon as they are made. Use plastic wrap to wrap the pan with the baked crust well and keep at room temperature until you make the cheesecake batter.

Even if a recipe calls for half a batch of the crust, make the full recipe and freeze half for the next time you make the same recipe, or for sprinkling over ice cream or pudding.

Note: the Gingersnap Cookie Crust on page 21 makes just enough to line the bottom of the pan, so for that recipe you'll need only step one of these instructions.

> *Golden Wisdom:* The time to line the bottom of the cheesecake pan with a parchment paper circle and butter the sides is now, before making the crust.

HOW TO LINE A PAN WITH COOKIE-CRUMB CRUST

Step 1 (bottom): Spoon half the crust mix (all the mix if you're using the Gingersnap Cookie Crust or another recipe that calls for lining the bottom only) into a 9-inch preferably nonstick springform pan, making a more or less even layer. Wrap the bottom of a short heavy glass, like the one Blanche used to make a Sloe Gin Fizz for Dr. Clayton, with plastic wrap. Lightly tamp down the crust mix into an even, packed layer. Patch up any holes if necessary.

Step 2 (sides): Spoon the remaining mix evenly around the edges of the pan. Using the sides of the same glass, roll and press the crumbs around the edges against the sides of the pan until the crust is pretty much the same height all around the sides and evenly packed. To finish off the sides, tilt the glass very slightly toward the side of the pan and keep rolling—this will pack the sides nicely and keep them in place during baking. If the crust is higher in some parts than others, don't obsess—it's all good. Bake the crust right away according to the instructions in that particular crust recipe.

Golden Wisdom: Why bake a crust? Baking adds to the flavor, and if you plan on keeping the finished cake for a few days, baking will help prevent the crust from getting soggy. Ditto if you're freezing and defrosting the cake before serving. Most of the work in fashioning a crust goes into making the crust itself and carefully lining the pan. Why not pop it in the oven for a few minutes to bake while you're arranging your gummy bear army around your bed?

Bake the crust directly on the middle rack. (See individual recipes for timing.) Remove and cool. If you bake the crust just before you make the cheesecake—as opposed to up to a day in advance—the time it takes to make the batter is enough time for the crust to cool.

Graham Cracker Crust

MAKES 2½ CUPS,
ENOUGH TO GENEROUSLY LINE THE BOTTOM AND SIDES OF A 9-INCH SPRINGFORM PAN

It's the quintessential cheesecake crust: buttery, sweet, and rich with graham cracker flavor. This can be paired with just about any cheesecake but goes best with mild-flavored cheesecakes like Dorothy's Straight Outta Brooklyn Creamy Cheesecake (page 50).

10 ounces regular or gluten-free graham crackers (about 18 whole crackers) or 2½ cups graham cracker crumbs (see variation below)

¼ cup granulated sugar

¼ teaspoon salt

1 stick (8 tablespoons) unsalted butter, melted and cooled

Heat the oven to 350°F with a rack in the center position. Crumble the graham crackers into a large food processor. Add the sugar and salt and process until the crackers are finely ground. Add the melted butter and process until the butter is completely mixed in and the crumb mixture looks like fine wet sand. Stop the processor a few times before and after adding the butter to scrape down the sides and bottom of the work bowl.

Line the bottom and sides, if applicable, of the pan with crust as described on page 15 Bake directly on the oven rack for 10 minutes and cool completely before filling.

Graham Cracker Crumb Variation: Put the crumbs, sugar, and salt in a medium bowl. Rub them together with your hands until very well mixed. Drizzle the butter over the crumbs and keep rubbing until the mix looks like fine wet sand. Bake and cool as above.

Chocolate Cookie Crust

MAKES ABOUT 2¼ CUPS,
ENOUGH TO LINE THE BOTTOM AND SIDES OF A 9-INCH SPRINGFORM PAN

Super chocolaty and borderline crisp—a good thing—this is just as simple to make as a traditional graham cracker crust. This recipe calls for a full package of cookies, but that allows for the two to three cookies you're bound to eat while making it.

One 9-ounce package Nabisco Famous Chocolate Wafers

2 tablespoons sugar

¼ teaspoon salt

6 tablespoons butter, melted and cooled

Heat the oven to 350°F with a rack in the center position. Crumble the cookies into a large food processor. Add the sugar and salt and process until the cookies are finely ground, at least 2 minutes. Add the melted butter and process until the butter is completely mixed in and the crumb mixture looks like fine wet sand. Stop the processor a few times before and after adding the butter to scrape down the sides and bottom of the work bowl.

Line the bottom and sides, if applicable, of the pan with crust as described on page 15. Bake directly on the oven rack for 8 minutes. Cool completely before filling.

ROSE: *What rhymes with "orange"?*

DOROTHY: *Cheesecake?*

ROSE: *"Orange Cheesecake." "Orange Cheese-cake." I suppose that could work.*

DOROTHY: *I meant to eat, Rose.*

Vanilla Wafer Crust

MAKES 3 CUPS,
ENOUGH TO LINE THE BOTTOM AND SIDES OF A 9-INCH SPRINGFORM PAN

There is no way to mistake the flavor of this crust—it's pure vanilla wafer through and through. In addition to the sweet and mellow taste that brings out the kid in everyone, this crust is surprisingly sturdy, making it a good choice for cakes that will be made two to three days in advance.

One 11-ounce box vanilla wafers

2 tablespoons sugar

¼ teaspoon salt

3 tablespoons butter, melted and cooled

Heat the oven to 350°F with a rack in the center position. Remove 8 to 10 cookies from the box. (These are for nibbling on while the cheesecake is baking or while watching *The Golden Girls* episodes.) Put about half the remaining cookies in a food processor and blitz until finely chopped. Put the rest of the cookies and the sugar and salt into the food processor and process to fine crumbs, scraping down the sides of the work bowl once or twice. Pour in the butter and process until the crumbs look like fine damp sand. (This crust isn't as moist as others, but it will hold its shape before and after baking.) Scrape down the bowl one more time and process a few seconds for good measure.

Line the bottom and sides, if applicable, of the pan with crust as described on page 15 Bake directly on the oven rack for 10 minutes. Cool completely before filling.

Gingersnap Cookie Crust

MAKES ABOUT 1⅓ CUPS, ENOUGH TO LINE THE BOTTOM OF A 9-INCH SPRINGFORM PAN

This is a flavorful crust, so keep it to just the bottom of the pan, not the sides. The spicy, gingery flavor means it won't pair well with all cheesecakes, but it's a hands-down winner for Rose's *The Fall of St. Olaf* Pumpkin Cheesecake (page 76). If you love gingersnaps, try this crust with Straight Outta Brooklyn Creamy Cheesecake (page 50), Key Lime Cheesecake Squares (page 59), or, if you know your crowd, Double Fudge Chocolate Cheesecake (page 52).

20 gingersnap cookies (about 5 ounces)

2 tablespoons butter, melted and cooled

2 tablespoons light or dark brown sugar

¼ teaspoon salt

Heat the oven to 350°F with a rack in the center position. Put the gingersnaps in a heavy sealable plastic bag and whack them around until they are finely crumbled. (Resist the urge to lay into them with a melon baller.) Put the broken-up cookies in a food processor and process until finely ground. This may take a few minutes. Add the butter, brown sugar, and salt and process until the mixture is blended and feels like fine wet sand.

Press the crust mix into the bottom of a 9-inch springform pan as described on page 15 Bake directly on the oven rack for 8 minutes. Cool completely before filling.

Baked Sugar Cookie Crust

This delicately flavored, easy-to-make crust allows the flavor of a cheesecake to shine through and also makes a sturdy base for moister cheesecakes. A sugar cookie crust can be used for just about every cheesecake in this book, but it is particularly good with the Double Fudge Amaretto Ricotta Cheesecake (page 132) and the Cannoli Cheesecake (p 139). A nutty version is part of the Chocolate Macadamia Nut Cheesecake on page 87.

¾ cup plus 2 tablespoons all-purpose flour

¼ teaspoon baking powder

5 tablespoons butter, at room temperature (but not too soft)

¼ cup granulated sugar

1 egg

1 teaspoon pure vanilla extract

Sift the flour and baking powder into a bowl. In a separate bowl and using a hand mixer, beat the butter and sugar on medium speed until thoroughly blended. Beat in the egg and vanilla, stopping once or twice to scrape down the bowl, until completely smooth. Switch to a rubber spatula and stir in the flour mixture until thoroughly blended. The dough can be made up to 2 days in advance and refrigerated. Bring to room temperature before continuing.

Press the dough more or less evenly into the bottom of a 9-inch springform pan. Cover the bottom of a heavy glass with plastic wrap and use this to pat/press the dough into an even layer to cover the bottom of the pan right up to the edges. Poke the dough all over with a fork and chill 20 to 30 minutes.

Heat the oven to 350°F with a rack in the center position. Bake right on the oven rack for 15 minutes. Rotate the pan back to front and continue baking until the edges are golden brown and the top is light brown, 6 to 8 minutes. Cool completely before using. Store the baked crust in the pan, wrapped tightly in plastic wrap, for up to 1 day.

Golden Wisdom: Feeling nutty? Add ¼ cup of your favorite toasted nut, finely chopped, to the flour and toss before adding the flour to the dough.

TOPPINGS

Yes, cheesecake is delicious, and, yes, it is the answer to all life's problems. So can it get any better than that?

Yes again—by topping it with any of the fruity, creamy, caramelly toppings below. There are no rules for mixing and matching toppings with cakes and crusts. Generally speaking, the simpler the cake, the more you can do with the toppings.

Switching out the guava topping on Guava Cheesecake at Midnight with a cherry topping? Good.

Piling dulce de leche on top of a key lime cheesecake square made with chocolate crust? Not so good. Unless you think it is.

Dulce de Leche

Three hours may seem like a long time to make a cheesecake topping, but when you consider that about 98 percent of that time the sweetened condensed milk is doing its own thing, it's really a breeze. Once the can is simmering away, you're free to test your Vacuum Slacks, relax with your heatin' pad, or whip up a batch of zabaglione. Please read all the instructions and cautions before you start.

One to three 14-ounce cans sweetened condensed milk

Remove the labels and give the cans a good washing to remove as much of the adhesive as possible. Put the cans in a pot large enough to hold them comfortably and with at least 3 inches headroom. Pour in enough water to cover by 2 inches and heat to boiling. Adjust the heat to a bare simmer and cook 3 hours. Make sure there is enough water to cover the cans by at least 1 inch at all times. Top off with hot water as necessary. A good rule of thumb is to check the water level every 20 to 30 minutes.

At the end of the 3-hour cooking time, leave the cans in the water until the water is barely warm to the touch. Don't even go *near* a finished can of dulce de leche with a can opener until it is completely cooled, at least 4 hours after it comes out of the pot.

Golden Wisdom: Each 14-ounce can of sweetened condensed milk makes about 1½ cups of finished dulce de leche. But if you're going to go, *go big* and make two or three cans at once. Heads up, survivalists: unopened cans of finished dulce can be stored on the pantry shelf for months—no need to refrigerate.

Ganache

Super chic, and so easy even cousin Sven could make it, ganache is a fancy name for rich chocolate glaze that's as at home on a cheesecake as it is on a bowl of vanilla ice cream.

6 ounces bittersweet (70%) chocolate

¾ cup heavy cream

Break up the chocolate into a small heatproof bowl. Heat the heavy cream in a small saucepan just until bubbles form around the edges. Pour the cream over the chocolate and let stand for a minute. Whisk until the ganache is smooth and shiny and all the chocolate has melted. That's it; you're done.

Pour it warm over a whole, thoroughly chilled cheesecake (with no side crust) and let it run down the sides in thick drips, or let it cool until thick enough to spread and slather over the top before slicing. If you're jonesing for a spreadable, slightly fluffy frosting or topping, whip the room temperature ganache with a hand mixer or stand mixer with the whip attachment until creamy and spreadable. Yum.

I said, Yum.

Sour Cream or Mascarpone Topping

MAKES ABOUT 1 CUP,
ENOUGH TO TOP ONE 9-INCH CHEESECAKE

A must for Sophia's Double Fudge Amaretto Ricotta Cheesecake (page 132), but also very nice on any cheesecake where a little tang would be welcome.

1 cup sour cream or mascarpone

3 tablespoons sugar

½ teaspoon vanilla extract

Whisk all ingredients together in a bowl just until the sugar is dissolved. Be careful not to overwhip, or, if using, the mascarpone may curdle. Refrigerate until needed, then spread over the top of the chilled cheesecake. This topping can be made while the cheesecake is baking or cooling.

Raspberry Sauce for Drizzling

MAKES ABOUT ¾ CUP

Don't limit the drizzling to cheesecake. Try this over ice cream or pound cake, too. The bold red sauce makes an even more dramatic entrance when drizzled over a dollop of whipped cream that sits atop a cheesecake slice.

One 9-ounce package frozen raspberries, defrosted

1½ to 2 tablespoons sugar

Lemon juice as needed

Pour the raspberries and their liquid into a blender. Blend on low speed just until smooth. Strain into a small heavy saucepan to remove the seeds. Add sugar to taste and heat to simmering. Stir until the sugar is dissolved. Cool to room temperature, then stir in lemon juice to taste. The raspberry sauce will keep refrigerated for up to 2 weeks.

Crushed Raspberry Whipped Cream

MAKES 2 CUPS

Whipped cream with bright streaks of ruby red raspberries can be served with just about any cheesecake. It is pretty, not too sweet, and super easy to make.

1 pint raspberries

1 tablespoon confectioners' sugar

1 cup heavy cream

Using a fork, coarsely mash the raspberries with the confectioners' sugar in a medium bowl. If you have the time, let sit at room temperature for 1 hour or so. Whip the heavy cream in a chilled bowl until it holds stiff peaks. Gently fold the raspberries and their liquid into the whipped cream, just until streaky—don't overfold. The topping can be refrigerated for an hour or two.

Guava Topping

Guava paste has a rich, deeply fruity taste. This topping can double as a filling for layer cake, a topping for pound cake, or even as layers in an ice cream parfait.

12 ounces guava paste, cut into cubes

½ lemon, juiced

Pinch salt

Put the guava paste cubes and ⅓ cup water in a small saucepan over medium heat. Mash with a potato masher or large fork until the mixture is spreadable but not completely smooth. Remove the pan from heat and stir in the lemon juice and salt. Cool for 15 to 20 minutes.

Pineapple Topping

Pineapple topping is mandatory for the Piña Colada Cheesecake on page 140. All this pineapple-y goodness also makes a delectable layer cake filling . . . or glaze for a baked ham. (If ham is on the menu, make the glaze long enough in advance that it is chilled when you spread it onto the ham for the last half hour of cooking.)

2 cups pineapple pieces (not too big)

2 tablespoons sugar

Pinch salt

2 tablespoons pineapple vodka, light rum, or water

1 teaspoon cornstarch

Up to four hours before serving the cake, make the topping. Pulse the pineapple in a food processor until crushed—not too chunky and not too fine. Scrape the pineapple into a wide skillet and stir in the sugar and salt. Bring to a full boil, then lower the heat to a gentle boil. Cook for 10 minutes, stirring occasionally.

Stir the vodka, rum, or water together with the cornstarch until the cornstarch is dissolved. Stir the cornstarch slurry into the pineapple and cook until thickened, 1 to 2 minutes. Cool the pineapple topping completely. Spoon room-temperature topping over slices of cheesecake when serving, or spread the cooled topping on the entire chilled cheesecake and refrigerate at least 30 minutes and up to several hours.

(Frozen) Fruit Toppings

It's the iconic image of a cheesecake—pale yellow, tall, wrapped in a graham cracker crust and piled high with fruit topping. If you feel that your cheesecake would shine with a fruit topping—whatever type of cheesecake it is—go ahead with one of these beautiful toppings.

Fruit can vary in sweetness and moisture, and people can vary as to how thick they like a topping, so use the amounts below as a guideline and tweak along the way.

Fruit toppings are most dramatic (and delicious) when spooned at room temperature over chilled cheesecake. The syrupy goodness will drip deliciously down the sides of each slice. Or you can spoon it over the cheesecake and let it set up in the refrigerator before serving.

NOTE: Frozen fruits are used for these toppings because they are available year-round, hold up well to the brief cooking and are, as a rule, very flavorful. Bags of frozen fruit vary in size, so cup measurements are given for each. If you have a little more or a little less, there's no need to worry.

Each topping makes about 1⅓ to 1½ cups, enough to top a 9-inch cheesecake.

All fruit toppings are made by following the same steps. The amounts of sugar, cornstarch, and water may vary from fruit to fruit, so suggestions for amounts of these ingredients as well as little additions unique to that topping are given in each mini recipe.

Here are the steps:

* Toss the frozen fruit and the lesser amount of sugar together in a deep-ish 10-inch (or so) skillet. Toss gently until the fruit is completely defrosted and the juice is syrupy.

* Heat the fruit-sugar mix over medium heat until gently simmering. Meanwhile, stir the cornstarch and water together until smooth.

* When the fruit is bubbling, stir in about ⅔ of the cornstarch slurry and simmer until thickened. If you'd like the mixture thicker (see Golden Wisdom on the next page), stir in the rest of the slurry.

* Taste and add some/all of the remaining sugar.

* Scrape the topping into a bowl and cool to room temperature before using.

* Spoon the topping over a chilled cheesecake and nudge it toward the edges with a large spoon.

Cherry Topping

One 12-ounce bag frozen
dark sweet cherries
(3 scant cups)

1½ to 2 tablespoons sugar

2 teaspoons cornstarch

1 tablespoon water

½ teaspoon vanilla extract,
optional

Make the topping as described above and stir in the vanilla, if using, just after removing the topping from the heat.

Blueberry Topping

One 10-ounce bag frozen
blueberries, about
2½ cups

2 to 3 tablespoons sugar

2 tablespoons water

1½ teaspoons cornstarch

1 lemon, optional

Make the topping as described above. When thickened and sweetened to your taste, grate a little zest from the lemon, if using, and squeeze a little of the juice in as well.

Mango Topping

16 ounces frozen mango chunks or cubes (3 generous cups; see note)

2 to 3 tablespoons sugar

1 tablespoon water

1½ teaspoons cornstarch

1 lime, optional

Make the topping as described above. When thickened and sweetened to your taste, grate a little zest from the lime, if using, and squeeze a little of the juice in as well.

Note: Frozen mango cubes can vary in size from brand to brand and even within the same bag. Cut them all into the same bite-size pieces while they are still frozen, if you can, or when defrosted if you can't.

Golden Wisdom: Here's a simple test to determine if a topping is thick enough for your taste. After adding part of the cornstarch mix, spoon a tablespoon or so of liquid into a small glass bowl and refrigerate the bowl for a few minutes. If the glaze is too thin for your liking, add the rest of the cornstarch slurry and reheat to boiling.

BLANCHE: *You know what would go so good on this cheesecake is those chocolate sprinkles.*

ROSE: *We finished those an hour ago.*

DOROTHY: *We could crush some Oreos on top.*

ROSE: *We ran out of those two hours ago.*

DOROTHY: *How about some whipped cream?*

BLANCHE: *Mm! I think we still have a can. I'll get it. It's in my bedroom.*

DOROTHY: *Never mind, Blanche.*

TRIMMINGS

* Lightly sweetened or unsweetened whipped cream, dolloped on with a spoon for a casual look, or piped into rosettes with a pastry bag and star tip.

* Sprinkles look their best when sprinkled on top of dollops of whipped cream.

* Use a vegetable peeler to shave any type of chocolate over the top of the cheesecake. Choose a large(ish) piece of chocolate and use a wadded paper towel to hold the chocolate so it won't melt in your hand.

* Drizzles of melted bittersweet, semi-sweet, or milk chocolate.

* Berries! Make a ring of fresh raspberries, blackberries, or sliced strawberries about the edge of the cake. Or plant individual berries atop small rosettes of whipped cream.

CHEESECAKE BAKING TIPS

* *Do not* buy a cheesecake pan from the 99¢-or-less bin. A good-quality nonstick 9-inch springform pan will set you back about fifteen bucks, less than two hours' work at Dorothy's rate of $8 an hour. (However many drachmas that works out to be . . .)

* To make moving the cheesecake easier, cut a parchment paper circle that fits over the bottom of the pan. Put the parchment circle in place before you make the crust or pour in the batter. To move the chilled cake, slide a long thin spatula between paper and pan, then slide in another metal spatula to help lift the cake. Make sure the cake is *completely* chilled, as in overnight chilled, before attempting to move it.

* Butter the sides of the pan even if it is a nonstick pan. If the cake sticks to the sides of the pan, it may crack as it cools.

* If you think making cheesecake, or any other cake, might become your thing, invest in cake circles, available at baking supply stores and craft stores. These corrugated cardboard circles make transporting cheesecake a breeze. It's also a good idea to use a cake circle when serving a cake directly from a cake stand or serving platter to prevent scratches to the stand or platter. Choose 9-inch circles for all cakes in this book.

* Slow baking the cheesecake in a deepish roasting pan partially filled with hot water, aka a "water bath" (page 38), is one of the keys to cheesecake happiness. Choose the right size roasting pan for the water bath; the pan should hold the cake pan comfortably with at least an inch all the way around the pan. Inexpensive 11 × 13-inch (or similar size) roasting pans will do the trick. Nothing fancy needed here.

* Bring cream cheese, eggs, and any other room temperature ingredients called for to true room temperature before starting to mix. Figure about 2 hours for cream cheese and about 1 hour for eggs. Unwrapping the cream cheese and putting it in the mixing bowl will move things along a little.

* When beating the cream cheese and sugar together, be sure the mix is free of lumps before adding the other ingredients. Once egg or any other liquid is added, it is virtually impossible to get rid of lumps.

* When in doubt, scrape! Stop to scrape down the bowl a few times when beating the cream cheese and sugar and then again when adding the eggs or other liquid ingredients, and yet again when adding other ingredients, like nuts or chocolate chips. And the last thing to do before scraping the batter into the pan is to give the bowl one last big scrape to be sure the batter is completely mixed.

* Wetter batters, like the Banana Pudding Cheesecake (page 60) or the Double Fudge Amaretto Ricotta Cheesecake (page 132), should be baked a little longer and until firmer in the center than other cheesecakes. Guidelines for baking and testing are in the recipes. Even though these cakes bake longer, their higher moisture content means they will still be creamy.

* Lastly, never, ever take your cheesecake to someone's house while it is still on the metal bottom of the springform pan. The bottom of the pan will disappear, never to be seen again. Scientists and specialists in paranormal events have been trying to figure this one out for years.

COOLING, CHILLING, AND SERVING CHEESECAKE

* Once the cake passes the doneness test outlined in the recipe, turn off the oven and leave the oven door open just a crack, 3 to 4 inches or so (unless the recipe states otherwise). Let the cake sit inside until the oven itself is completely cool, about an hour.

* Remove the cake from the water bath (it will still be quite warm) and move it to a cooling rack. Let it cool to a true room temperature. This can take as long as 2 to 3 hours.

* After cooling, gently run a thin paring knife around the edges to make sure the cake hasn't stuck in places. Remove the foil, unclasp the side of the pan, and carefully lift from the cake. Put the cake in the refrigerator.

* Chill the cake at least 6 hours before slicing. Overnight is better. Cover lightly with plastic wrap after 2 hours or so.

* To serve, set up a container of hot water near the cake and use it to dip the knife after each slice. If your cheesecake has a topping, a damp wad of paper towels alongside the water is a good idea.

* All cheesecakes can be frozen. Some hold up better than others, though. A general rule of thumb: the firmer the cheesecake is going into the freezer, the better it will hold up. Defrost frozen cheesecake in the refrigerator for several hours and up to overnight.

DON'T CRACK UP!

The tops of cheesecakes sometimes crack, most often for these three main reasons:

The batter is beaten too much, incorporating air, which causes the cake to rise more than it should and then crack when it collapses. To prevent this, use medium-low mixer speeds for the initial creaming of the cream cheese and sugar. If you have a choice between a good hand mixer and a stand mixer, opt for the hand mixer, which will most likely incorporate less air. For added protection against cracks, once the heavy mixing is done, abandon the machine and switch to a handheld whisk. Gently whisk in the remaining ingredients just until blended into the batter. Recipes where this is strongly suggested have details for switching to a whisk or rubber spatula and using "manual power."

The top of the cake is too dry, caused by too-high oven temperature or baking too long. Invest in an oven thermometer to make sure your oven is running at the correct temperature. Most cheesecakes call for baking the cakes on the center rack in a water bath as described on page 38. (Cupcakes and cheesecake squares are the exception.) Keep a kettle full of water hot over low heat while making the batter and use it to fill the water bath with hot water that reaches about 1 inch up the sides of the cake pan. In addition to helping the cheesecake cook evenly, a water bath will keep moisture in the oven high during baking.

The cheesecake cooled too quickly. To avoid this, leave cheesecakes in the turned-off oven with the door only slightly ajar for a full hour or until the oven is cool. Cupcakes and cheesecake squares don't need such gentle cooling, but slower is better for those as well.

There is a slight chance your cheesecake will crack even if you've followed all these steps. **Above all, promise me you won't fret none if the cake cracks!** For an easy fix, spoon one of the toppings (pages 23 through 32) over the top to hide the cracks. Or just march out that door and serve the whole cheesecake, cracks and all, unapologetically!

 BLANCHE: *We're gonna march out that door right now, like the strong confident women I know we are. Chins up, chests out, buttocks tight. I know "buttocks tight" has nothing to do with it, it just looks good.*

PREPARE YOUR PAN FOR A WATER BATH

Cut a 12-inch length of extra-wide (18-inch) aluminum foil. Put the pan in the center of the foil and bring the foil up around the sides of the pan. Work your way around the overlap where the pan bottom fits into the sides—i.e., where water is likely to leak in—crimping the foil tightly against the sides and bottom of the pan as you go. Make sure the pan sits level before you put the cake in the oven. If it doesn't, crimp the foil along the bottom as needed.

ROSE: *Why do people die, Dorothy?*

DOROTHY: *Oh, please, Rose. I don't even know why fools fall in love!*

ROSE: *I killed her. I might just as well have shot her with a gun.*

DOROTHY: *Honey, the woman was eighty-three. She had a heart attack. It was just a coincidence. Now, you haven't slept for two nights. You have to stop torturing yourself.*

ROSE: *I guess you're right.*

BLANCHE *[entering]: Oh, Rose, honey, you can't sleep again?*

ROSE: *No.*

BLANCHE: *Oh, Rose, you have to put this terrible thing behind you. You killed Mrs. Claxton two days ago.*

Cocktails

The first rule of cocktail making at home is this: *Keep it simple*. This isn't *Cocktail* the movie, and chances are you're not Tom Cruise. (If you are, get ready to peel Sophia off the ceiling!) These are simple recipes, easy to re-create with just a few pieces of equipment you probably already have.

WHAT YOU'LL NEED

INGREDIENTS

Ice is essential to a well-made cocktail, mocktail, or any cool beverage. If you have an ice maker in your fridge, you're all set. If not, make or buy the biggest ice cubes possible. They melt slower, and that's a good thing. Some drink recipes call for crushed ice. If your ice maker dispenses crushed ice, again, you're all set. Many blenders have a crushed ice setting; use that if it's an option. If not, put ice cubes in a double-thick heavy plastic bag and whack with a small mallet or sturdy rolling pin until coarsely crushed. Put the whole bag in the freezer until needed.

Citrus Juices—lemon, orange, lime, and, in the case of the Sloe Gin Fizz with a Kick, yuzu—add zip and freshness to many of these recipes. Squeeze them ahead and refrigerate as part of your bar setup, but not too far ahead. They'll feel a little flat if left to sit more than a couple of hours. Whether you squeeze halved citrus with a reamer,

electric juicer, or citrus squeezer, don't push too hard—the white rind of citrus has a bitter tang.

Simple Syrup is a breeze to make, lasts forever in the fridge, and mixes easily in everything from lemonade (see Rose's Rose-Colored Lemonade, page 101) to the New Fashioned on page 68. Simple syrup can also be infused with ginger and orange (see page 93), strips of citrus zest, chili peppers, and just about anything else you like in your cocktails. A couple of recipes call for muddling a sugar cube with things like orange slices or mint leaves as the base of a cocktail. This is mostly for effect, and a nice effect it is, but if you're fresh out of sugar cubes, simple syrup will do the trick.

To make 1 cup of simple syrup, stir 1 cup sugar and 1 cup water together in a small saucepan over medium-low heat to simmering. (This amount is simple to scale up or down.) Stir just until all the sugar is dissolved and remove the pan from the heat. Refrigerate indefinitely.

EQUIPMENT

Cocktail Sets come in all shapes and sizes. A three-piece shaker set with a sturdy metal cup, strainer lid, and cap is all you really need. But look for a set that includes a jigger and a cocktail spoon. Both are nice to have, but not essential. There are smaller sizes of shakers for making one cocktail, and slightly larger models for making two. Choose the one that suits you best.

A few basic shapes and sizes of **Glasses**, which are probably already in your cupboard, are all you'll need for most drinks. A short wide glass, also known as a rocks glass or Old Fashioned glass, is just right for drinks served on the rocks, a simple splash of bourbon or the like, or a shorter pour of lemonade. Two options for drinks served shaken and "up" (without ice) are the coupe and classic cocktail or martini

glass. If going for the latter, pick one of a smaller size, not the overly large versions that one sometimes finds. Tall glasses are perfect for lemonade, many nonalcohol drinks, and drinks served with mixers over ice. And don't forget champagne flutes. Just because.

No way around it, frozen drinks need a **Blender**. They range in price from $39 or so to as high as $600. (That's more than the original down payment on Blanche's first house!) If in the market for a new blender, pick one with a crushed-ice setting. That'll come in handy when making nonfrozen cocktails, too.

Use a **Muddler** to smash and extract flavor from ingredients that form the base of a cocktail. Among the drinks that start with

a muddler are The Big Daddy (page 127; sugar and mint are muddled) and Dorothy's New Fashioned (page 68; blueberry and orange). Or come up with your own muddled creations as Rose did with her Muddled Gin and Tonic (page 96; cucumber and salt). Although it should be said that Rose might have mistaken cucumber slices for lime wedges. If you come from St. Olaf, you do things like that.

Measuring Tools can be the everyday measuring cups and spoons you already own or bar jiggers with ounce measurements marked on the inside of the cup. Jiggers are easier to use and are sometimes included in basic cocktail-making starter sets. But measuring spoons will do in a pinch. All cocktail recipes list ingredients in both ounces and tablespoons (1 ounce = 2 tablespoons).

Have Some Fun! Colorful straws, little umbrellas, plastic monkeys that hang off the sides of a glass, long wooden picks to spear citrus wedges—you get the idea.

THE GOLDEN GIRLS GUIDE TO DRINK GARNISHES

CITRUS

TWISTS

Using a vegetable peeler, remove a strip of citrus zest about 1 inch wide and 2 inches long. Exact size doesn't matter. Press lightly on the peeler so only the outer layer of the peel (zest) is removed without digging into the white pith below. Before serving, and this is where the "twist" comes in, twist the citrus strip over the drink and drop it in. If you look closely, you will see tiny beads of oil being released from the zest—these are very flavorful and make a difference in the drink.

WEDGES AND CUBES

Think of these as little chunks of flavor and juice. Cut the citrus in question into wedges, remove the white membrane from the tapered end of the wedge, and use as is. Or trim the ends of the wedge and cut in half crosswise to make cubes before dropping into the drink. Whether to squeeze the wedge into the drink is up to you.

SLICES

Cut a ½-inch or so slice from the center two-thirds of the fruit. Cut that in half and poke out the seeds if necessary. To make bartending life a little easier, cut a notch in the slice and use the notch to hang it on the side of the glass.

FRUIT AND VEGETABLES

SKEWERS

Find nice 3-inch or so decorative bamboo or wooden skewers and keep them near your bar area. Thread the appropriate fruit onto the skewer and lay the skewer across the top of the glass before serving. If serving the drink in a tall glass, you may choose to drop the skewer into the glass. In the case of the cucumber ribbons (page 96), thread them onto the skewer going back and forth to make an accordion pattern. Here are a few suggestions: thread a few cubes of citrus on a skewer; alternate maraschino cherries and orange cubes, or pineapple and cherries, or chunks of cucumber and cubes of lime, or . . .

FREE-FORM

Just drop the fruit into the glass. In a tall glass, drop in one citrus wedge or cube when the glass is about half full and another one on the top to add a little zip to the look. Same for cherries, pineapple cubes, and cucumber slices.

> **DOROTHY:** *Do you know how many problems we have solved over a cheesecake at this kitchen table?*
> **ROSE:** *No, Dorothy. Exactly how many?*
> **DOROTHY:** *A hundred and forty-seven, Rose!*

Dorothy

PURSUING A CAREER in education requires the right amount of patience, gusto, and ambition. And that's how we picture a young Dorothy Zbornak developing the recipes she no doubt would keep in an organized notebook.

After first setting her dessert goals, she lays out her approach to creating, first heading out to the market to gather what's needed. Armed with a few simple ingredients, a springform pan, and a hand mixer, Dorothy uses her prodigious mental skills to create a cheesecake that gets tens across the board from all and sundry, including her feisty Sicilian mother, who is known to speak her mind. The cheesecake is rich and creamy with just the right amount of tang. Even Stan, her sex-crazed nudnik of a baby daddy, approves!

But why stop there? Inspired by *the* Petrillo family recipe for cheesecake, Dorothy improvises on her creation, blending melted chocolate into the batter for a dense, ultra-chocolaty version. Should we call this the Zbornak Zpecial?

Emboldened by her success, she moves on to transforming a favorite comfort food, banana pudding, into a layered cheesecake concoction that takes her Brooklyn neighborhood by storm. Even Jeanette Pasadano, who owns the little candy store down the street, has nothing but rave reviews!

And to add zest in a snackable size: lime cheesecake squares. Even Dorothy knows she has reached the heights of cheesecake notoriety when her brother Phil goes to town on tasty square without any concern for the crumbs he might get on his brand-new culottes.

In addition to the learning we do every day, Dorothy can impart upon us a new definition of ABCs: Always Bake Cheesecakes.

Straight Outta Brooklyn Creamy Cheesecake

MAKES 16 SERVINGS

In a borough known for its New York–style cheesecake, one outshines them all. Not that Brooklyn institution that gets all the press, but Dorothy's version. It's as simple as a cheesecake gets, rich and creamy with just the right amount of tang from sour cream. Maybe Dorothy should open a cheesecake shop called "Seniors"?

Graham Cracker Crust (page 18) for bottom and sides of pan, baked

2 pounds cream cheese, at room temperature

1 cup plus 2 tablespoons sugar

4 teaspoons cornstarch

¼ teaspoon salt

3 large eggs, at room temperature

2 teaspoons vanilla extract

¾ cup sour cream

Heat the oven to 350°F with a rack in the center position. Prepare the springform pan for a water bath as described on page 38 and put it in a roasting pan. Keep a kettle of water hot over low heat.

Using a handheld mixer or stand mixer with the paddle attachment, beat the cream cheese, sugar, cornstarch, and salt together on medium-low speed just until creamy and lump-free, stopping a few times to scrape down the sides of the bowl. Beat in the eggs, adding them one at a time and stopping about halfway through to scrape down the bowl. Switch to low speed and beat in the vanilla and sour cream. Scrape down the bowl one last time to make sure the batter is evenly mixed.

Scrape the batter into the crust and gently wiggle the pan to even out the top. Pull out the oven rack, put the roasting pan on the rack, and pour in enough hot water to reach about 1 inch up the sides of the cake pan. Carefully slide the rack back in. Immediately lower the oven temperature to 300°F. Bake until about 2 inches around the edges of the cake are firm and the center is slightly jiggly, about 1 hour. (Don't check until at least 45 minutes into the baking.) Turn off the oven and leave the door slightly ajar. Cool, chill, and serve according to the Tips on page 36.

> *Options:* ✳ Substitute Chocolate Cookie Crust (page 19) or Vanilla Wafer Crust (page 20) for the graham cracker crust.
>
> ✳ Top with any of the toppings on pages 23–32.

Double Fudge Chocolate Cheesecake

MAKES 16 SERVINGS

A freezer stash of Double Fudge Chocolate Cheesecake certainly helped the girls get over the harrowing experience of watching *Psycho* together. That is, until a knife-wielding Sophia burst into the kitchen to freak them out all over again. You don't need to be scared silly to enjoy this cheesecake—just in the mood for a super-rich, super-chocolaty treat.

Chocolate Cookie Crust (page 19) for bottom and sides of pan, baked

1½ pounds cream cheese, at room temperature

1¼ cups granulated sugar

4 teaspoons cornstarch

¼ teaspoon salt

3 large eggs, at room temperature

8 ounces bittersweet chocolate (70%), melted and kept warm (see Golden Wisdom opposite)

¼ cup sour cream

1½ teaspoons vanilla extract

Heat the oven to 350°F with a rack in the center position. Prepare the springform pan for a water bath as described on page 38 and put it in a roasting pan. Keep a kettle of water hot over low heat.

Using a handheld mixer or a stand mixer with the paddle attachment, beat the cream cheese, sugar, cornstarch, and salt together on medium-low speed just until creamy and lump-free, stopping a few times to scrape down the bowl. Beat in the eggs, adding them one at a time and stopping halfway through to scrape down the bowl. Switch to low speed and mix in the warm chocolate, sour cream, and vanilla just until blended. Scrape down the bowl and stir well to make sure the batter is evenly mixed.

Scrape the batter into the crust and gently wiggle the pan to even out the top. Pull out the oven rack, put the roasting pan on it, and pour in enough hot water to reach about 1 inch up the sides of the cake pan. Carefully slide the rack back in. Immediately lower the oven temperature to 300°F. Bake until about 2 inches around the edges of the cake are firm and the center is slightly jiggly, about 1 hour to 1 hour and 10 minutes. (Don't check until at least 50 minutes into the baking.) Turn off the oven and leave the door slightly ajar. Cool, chill, and serve according to the Tips on page 36.

Options: ✳ Go totally over the top and top the cake with Ganache (whipped version, page 27).

✳ Go slightly over the top and top the cake with Sour Cream or Mascarpone Topping (page 27).

Golden Wisdom: Melt the chocolate in the microwave or a double boiler. Using a double boiler has the advantage of keeping the chocolate warm while the batter is being made.

To improvise a double boiler: Pour 1 to 2 inches of water into a small to medium saucepan. Choose a heatproof bowl that sits well above the water with most of the bottom of the bowl resting inside the sides of the saucepan. Do this before you start baking to avoid last-minute scrambling.

DOROTHY: *You know, there is nothing worse than being wide awake and scared and by yourself.*

ROSE: *Oh, yes there is! Being wide awake and scared and by yourself without a double-fudge chocolate cheesecake in the freezer.*

Magda's White Russian Cheesecake

MAKES 16 SERVINGS

It wasn't always smooth sailing when Stan's cousin Magda—aka Flora the Red Menace—paid the girls a visit. Pro-communist speeches, Slurpee-driven brain freeze, and a disruptive appearance at Blanche's sister Charmaine's book signing made for a rough week. But she did leave behind this recipe for cheesecake spiked with coffee liqueur and vanilla vodka and topped with coffee-infused whipped cream, just like a White Russian cocktail. The recipe is a treasured family heirloom. Magda got it from her grandmother, who slept with government official.

Softened butter for the pan

2 pounds cream cheese, at room temperature

1 cup sugar

1 tablespoon cornstarch

¼ teaspoon salt

4 large eggs, at room temperature

½ cup sour cream

¼ cup coffee liqueur

1 tablespoon vanilla vodka or 2 teaspoons vanilla extract

For the topping:

½ cup chilled heavy cream

1 teaspoon instant espresso powder

1 tablespoon sugar

Options:

* Spread 1 cup of room-temperature Dulce de Leche (page 26) over the top in place of the coffee whipped cream.

* Prepare and bake a Baked Sugar Cookie Crust (page 22) for the cheesecake.

Heat the oven to 325°F with a rack in the center position. Butter the bottom and sides of a 9-inch nonstick springform pan.

Prepare the springform pan for a water bath as described on page 38 and put it in a roasting pan. Keep a kettle of water hot over low heat.

Using a handheld or stand mixer with the paddle attachment, beat the cream cheese, sugar, cornstarch, and salt together on medium-low speed just until creamy and lump-free, stopping a few times to scrape down the bowl. Change the speed to low and beat in the eggs, adding them one at a time and stopping halfway through to scrape down the bowl. Switch to a whisk and beat in the sour cream, coffee liqueur, and vanilla vodka or vanilla extract by hand just until blended.

Scrape the batter into the pan and gently wiggle the pan to even out the top. Pull out the oven rack, put the roasting pan on the rack, and pour in enough hot water to reach about 1 inch up the sides of the cake pan. Carefully slide the rack back in. Immediately lower the oven temperature to 300°F. Bake until about 2 inches around the edges of the cake are firm and the center is slightly jiggly, about 1 hour and 15 minutes. (Don't check until at least 1 hour into the baking.) Turn off the oven and leave the door slightly ajar. Cool and chill according to the Tips on page 36.

Make the topping: Stir the cream and instant coffee together in a chilled bowl to dissolve the coffee. Add the sugar and whip with a handheld mixer or by hand until the cream holds medium-stiff peaks. Spread the topping over the cake and serve.

No-Bake Dulce de Leche Cheesecake Parfaits

MAKES 6 SERVINGS

Craving cheesecake but not the baking? These creamy, mousse-y layered parfaits are just the thing. If you are as organized and planful as Dorothy, you've already made an extra can of Dulce de Leche (page 26), and the parfaits can be made start to end in about 20 minutes.

12 (or so) thin chocolate cookies, such as Nabisco Famous Chocolate Wafers, or 16 vanilla wafer cookies

⅓ cup heavy cream

1 cup Dulce de Leche (page 26)

8 ounces cream cheese, at room temperature

2 tablespoons granulated sugar

1 teaspoon vanilla extract

1 tablespoon confectioners' sugar

Put the cookies in a sealable plastic bag and whack or roll them until as coarse or fine as you like. Beat the cream in a chilled bowl with a handheld mixer or with a whisk using "manual power" until it holds stiff peaks, but don't overbeat. Pop into the refrigerator until needed. Set aside 3 tablespoons of dulce de leche in a microwavable bowl. Scrape the rest into a mixing bowl or the bowl of a stand mixer. Add the cream cheese and sugar and beat together on medium-low speed just until creamy and lump-free, stopping twice to scrape down the bowl. Beat in the vanilla extract. Fold a scoop of the whipped cream into the dulce de leche mix to lighten it, then fold in the rest, scraping the bowl as you fold, just until no trace of white remains. Don't overfold.

Line up 6 parfait or tall wine glasses. Spoon about half the mixture into the glasses, dividing evenly. Sprinkle a thick layer of crumbs over the top of the mixture, using about half the crumbs. Repeat with the remaining mousse and crumbs. Heat the dulce de leche in a microwave in 5-second bursts just until warm enough to drizzle. Drizzle a little of the dulce over the tops of the parfaits. Chill at least 4 hours and up to 8 hours before serving.

Golden Wisdom: For a nicer presentation, tilt the glasses as you fill them so the dulce de leche mousse doesn't fill the glass straight across. Stand the glasses upright for the second layer of mousse and crumbs.

Key Lime Cheesecake Squares

MAKES 16 TWO-INCH SQUARES

Whip up a batch of these cheesecake squares next time you're in the mood for a quick cheesecake fix. They're tart with just the right amount of sweetness (remind you of anyone, Dorothy?) and the perfect light ending to a summer meal.

Softened butter for the pan

½ recipe Graham Cracker Crust (page 18)

8 ounces cream cheese, at room temperature

¼ teaspoon salt

One 14-ounce can sweetened condensed milk

3 egg yolks

⅓ cup freshly squeezed key lime juice or equivalent (see Golden Wisdom)

1½ teaspoons grated lime zest

Option: Swap out the graham cracker crust for Baked Sugar Cookie Crust (page 22).

Golden Wisdom: If you don't have access to fresh key limes, look for bottled key lime juice. If you strike out there as well, try this: substitute ¼ cup fresh lime juice plus 3 tablespoons fresh lemon juice for the key lime juice.

Heat the oven to 350°F with a rack in the center position. Butter the sides of an 8-inch square cake pan (even if it's nonstick). Cut a strip of parchment paper the width of the pan and long enough to reach at least the top edge of the pan. Crease the parchment so it fits neatly into the corners of the pan. The parchment will be used to lift the finished squares easily from the pan.

Make the half recipe of graham cracker crust and scrape it into the prepared pan. Tamp the crust into an even layer with the bottom of a glass wrapped with plastic wrap, making sure the parchment stays in place. Tamp the crust into the corners with your fingertips. Bake the crust for 10 minutes. Remove and cool while preparing the batter.

Heat the oven to 350°F with a rack in the center position. Using a handheld mixer, beat the cream cheese and salt together on medium-low speed just until creamy and lump-free. Continue mixing on medium-low speed while drizzling in the sweetened condensed milk. Scrape down the bowl and beat in the yolks on low speed. Scrape down the bowl again, then beat in the lime juice. Stir in the lime zest by hand, using a rubber spatula (so the zest doesn't get stuck in the beaters or paddle) and scraping the bowl as you go.

Scrape the batter over the crust and wiggle the pan to smooth the top. Bake until the batter is just barely wiggly, about 20 minutes. Turn off the oven, leave the door completely open, and cool 30 minutes. Remove the pan and cool on a rack to room temperature. Chill thoroughly, at least 4 hours and up to 1 day.

To serve, free the sides of the cheesecake with no parchment by running a very thin knife along them. Use the parchment handles to carefully lift the cheesecake onto a cutting board. Cut the cake into 2-inch squares (or whatever size and shape you like). Serve chilled.

Banana Pudding Cheesecake

MAKES 16 SERVINGS

When the girls need comfort food, they turn to cheesecake. When they *really* need comfort food, like after Rose killed Frieda Claxton, they turn to Banana Pudding Cheesecake.

One 11-ounce package mini vanilla wafers (see note below if using larger vanilla wafers)

Softened butter for the pan

2 medium bananas, ripe with a few brown spots

1 lemon

1½ pounds cream cheese, at room temperature

⅔ cup sugar

2 tablespoons cornstarch

¼ teaspoon salt

2 large eggs plus 2 yolks, at room temperature

¼ cup whole milk

2 teaspoons vanilla extract

Note: Mini wafers come in handy for making the middle layer and decorating the top of the cheesecake. If using regular vanilla wafers, make sure there is not too much space between them when layering into the cheesecake. Break up a few to fill any large gaps. To decorate the top, cut the larger wafers into quarters or just crumble them into large pieces.

Heat the oven to 350°F with a rack in the center position. Make a half recipe of Vanilla Wafer Crust (page 20) using half the box of wafers. Line the bottom only of a buttered 9-inch springform pan according to the directions on page 15, using a parchment paper circle if you like. Bake the crust for 10 minutes and cool while making the batter.

Heat the oven to 325°F. Butter the sides of the pan (again). Prepare the pan for a water bath according to directions on page 38 and put it in a roasting pan. Keep a kettle of water hot over low heat.

Peel the bananas and put them in a bowl. Zest 1 teaspoon of lemon into the bowl. Squeeze 2 teaspoons of lemon juice and add to the bowl. Mash the bananas to a smooth consistency, making about 1 cup. (Some small lumps are okay.) Set aside.

Using a handheld mixer or stand mixer with paddle attachment, beat the cream cheese, sugar, cornstarch, and salt together at medium-low speed just until creamy and lump-free. Add the eggs one at a time and then the yolks, stopping a few times to scrape down the bowl. Switch to a whisk and beat in the milk, vanilla, and mashed bananas by hand. Scrape the bowl to make sure the batter is well blended. Pour half the batter over the crust. Dip into the other half of the box of mini wafers to make a layer of wafers over the top, leaving a little space between them. Spoon, don't pour, the remaining batter over the wafers. Make a circle of mini wafers around the edge of the cheesecake and arrange a few more of them in the center if you like.

Pull out the oven rack, put the roasting pan on the rack, and pour in enough hot water to reach about 1 inch up the sides of the cake pan. Carefully slide the rack back in. Immediately lower the oven temperature to 300°F. Bake until about 3 inches of the cake around the edges are set and just the very center is still wiggly, about 1 hour and 10 minutes to 1 hour and 20 minutes. (Don't check until at least 1 hour into the baking.) Turn off the oven and leave the door slightly ajar. Cool, chill, and serve the cheesecake according to the Tips on page 36.

Gold Coast Cosmo

MAKES 1 COSMO (CAN SCALE UP AS NEEDED)

Bright like a Miami summer day, this version of a Cosmo swaps orange juice for cranberry. The other major players keep their roles, unlike Dorothy in the Miami Community Players' production of whatever-that-is-it's-not-really-*Picnic* starring Patrick Vaughn. Serve in a coupe with a half slice of orange.

1½ ounces (3 tablespoons) vodka

½ ounce (1 tablespoon) orange juice

½ ounce (1 tablespoon) not-too-sweet orange liqueur

1 or 2 lime wedges, for squeezing

½ orange slice, for garnish

Fill a small cocktail shaker two-thirds full of ice. Pour in the vodka, orange juice, and liqueur. Squeeze a lime wedge, or two if you like things tarter. (Guess which option Dorothy chooses.) Shake well and strain into a coupe or small cocktail glass. Garnish with the orange slice.

Neoclassic Margarita

MAKES ENOUGH MIX FOR 4 LARGE OR 6 REGULAR MARGARITAS

Dorothy always was one for the classics, both old and new: *The Sun Also Rises*, the *Odyssey, Beloved, Love in the Time of Cholera* . . . Dorothy's version of the Margarita combines both the traditional ingredients and a new twist—lime zest—in a tribute to Dorothy's thrifty, practical approach to life. Why not use some of the zest before juicing a lime rather than tossing it out?

3 to 4 limes, washed and thoroughly dried

1 cup good-quality tequila (silver, gold, or *reposado*)

½ cup not-too-sweet orange liqueur

Kosher salt

Lime wedges

Remove the zest from one and a half of the limes. Squeeze enough lime juice to measure ¼ cup. Cut one lime into wedges. Stir the tequila, orange liqueur, lime juice, and lime zest together in a small pitcher. Cover with plastic wrap and chill until needed, up to one day.

Just before serving, spread an even layer of kosher salt on a small plate. Rub the rims of coupes or small martini glasses with a wedge of lime and dip the edges in the salt. For two large or three small Margaritas: Fill a large cocktail shaker about two-thirds full of cracked ice. Pour in ¾ cup of the Margarita mix. Shake the Margarita vigorously until very frothy and ice cold. When you think you have shaken it enough, shake it another 5 to 10 seconds. Strain into the salt-rimmed glasses and serve immediately. Shake a little of the ice into each glass if you like. If you don't have a cocktail shaker and strainer, stir the Margarita mix and ice together vigorously for a minute or so in a tall glass with a bar spoon or iced tea spoon until very well chilled.

ROSE: *I have to tell you what happened. I died! I died and went to heaven!*

DOROTHY: *Rose, honey, you didn't die. You passed out. You hallucinated. Remember that New Year's Eve when you had the three Margaritas? Hmm? You thought you were an animated broom in Fantasia?*

Options: ✳ If yours is a spicy crowd, mix a large pinch of chili pepper into the salt before dipping the glasses into them.

✳ Shake the cocktails as described above, but pour the drinks with some of the ice into rocks or Old Fashioned glasses.

Not-Too-Sweet Piña Colada

MAKES 2 DRINKS

Craving the undeniably refreshing combo of pineapple and coconut in a Piña Colada but not the sticky-sweet vibe that usually comes with it? Use just a fraction of the cream of coconut in most versions and you'll still have enough coconut flavor and sweetness from the pineapple juice to make a bouncy cocktail.

3 ounces (generous ⅓ cup) pineapple juice

3 ounces (generous ⅓ cup) white rum

2 teaspoons cream of coconut

Pour the pineapple juice, rum, and cream of coconut into a large cocktail shaker filled with ice. Shake vigorously and strain into 2 coupes or small martini glasses. Garnish with a fruit skewer.

Options: ✳ Virgin Colada: Substitute 3 ounces orange juice for the rum. Shake and serve as above.

✳ Frozen Variation: Pour all ingredients into a blender. Add enough ice (crushed is nice) so the top of the liquid is even with the ice. Blend at high speed until slushy—how slushy is up to you. Serve in tall chilled glasses.

✳ Alternate pineapple cubes and maraschino cherries on a bamboo skewer for garnish.

New Fashioned

Sophia is partial to old-fashioned ways. Dorothy is the free, modern thinker who keeps up with the times. When bourbon whiskey made a big splashy comeback, Dorothy was right there, revitalizing an Old Fashioned with simple syrup instead of the sugar cube and doing away with the bottled cherry in favor of antioxidant-rich blueberries. Pick a bottle of newfangled bitters to keep up with the times.

½ orange slice

6 to 8 blueberries, fresh or frozen

1 teaspoon Simple Syrup (page 40)

A few drops of "new-fashioned" bitters (Dorothy recommends chocolate, orange, or cherry)

1½ ounces Kentucky bourbon or rye or Canadian whiskey

Muddle the orange slice, blueberry, simple syrup, and bitters in an Old Fashioned glass until the orange looks a little beat up. Drop in enough cracked ice to fill the glass halfway. Pour the bourbon over the ice, stir well, and serve.

Daiquiri

MAKES 1 DRINK (CAN SCALE UP AS NEEDED)

Dorothy's version of this classic is as far from the sugary poolside concoction as Dorothy is from having a good time at Mr. Ha Ha's Hot Dog Hacienda. And that's pretty far.

1½ to 2 ounces (3 to 4 tablespoons) light rum

1 ounce (2 tablespoons) freshly squeezed lime juice

½ to ¾ ounce (1 to 1½ tablespoons) Simple Syrup (page 40)

Lime twist

Fill a cocktail shaker two-thirds full of ice. Pour in the rum, lime juice, and simple syrup. Shake lazily until the outside of the shaker is very frosty. Strain into a coupe, twist the lime zest over the drink, and drop it in before serving.

Vodka and Black Underwear

MAKES 2 DRINKS

Dorothy, ever the hypochondriac, looks for any excuse to boost her chances of avoiding malady. She heard charcoal tablets are good for the stomach and kidneys. They're also used to relieve excess gas—maybe she should hand Sophia a few? Whether these claims are true or not, Dorothy is all over supplements, in her diet and in this cocktail.

1 ounce (2 tablespoons) vanilla or regular vodka

1 ounce (2 tablespoons) black sambuca

A few drops vanilla extract

1 capsule activated charcoal (about ⅛ teaspoon)

2 thin lemon slices

Fill a cocktail shaker two-thirds full of cracked ice. Pour in the vodka and sambuca. Drop in the vanilla extract and charcoal. Shake vigorously and strain into 2 coupes or small martini glasses. Notch the lemon slices and hang them off the side of the glasses.

BLANCHE *(discussing Marguerite the housekeeper): Girls, we can't fire her now. She's makin' me an aphrodisiac!*

DOROTHY: *Use vodka and black underwear like everyone else!*

DOROTHY: *Cheesecake, Rose?*
ROSE: *Let's taste it and find out!*

$\mathcal{R}$ose

BACK IN ST. OLAF... a sweetly dispositioned widow of Scandinavian descent decides to pick up and move to Miami.

Why?

Stop interrupting! She moves to Miami, okay?!

Although she lived in Miami on her own for quite some time, it was fate that she'd one day walk into a particular supermarket, with a particular stray cat, and meet a particular stranger looking for roommates. That cat is Mr. Peepers, and that cat-loving character is Rose Nylund.

73

Once ensconced in her new home, Rose starts to miss the domestic pastimes she left behind—knitting, baking, and listening to cousin Dat playing "Getting to Know You" through the hole in his windpipe. Her knitting needles may have been lost in the move, and cousin Dat may have moved toward the light, but, Jiminy Cricket, she can still bake!

She drives her car to that same unfamiliar supermarket to pick up supplies, but it is so much bigger than the St. Olaf market she knows so well! She gets lost and ends up in Dairy instead of Canned Foods, where she usually goes to collect her thoughts, such as they are.

"I know—cheesecake!" she exclaims while staring at the cream cheese (causing the stock boy to move a little further down the aisle). And just like that, a new tradition is born.

Rose takes a different approach to baking cheesecakes than most people. But, then again, Rose takes a different approach to life than most people. There's the Sunshine Cadet No-Bake Cheesecake Cupcakes studded with chocolate-cream cookies, or the one that has a mix of brownie batter and cheesecake batter, swirled together so every bite features a little of each. Or, no doubt created in a fit of whimsy, the one with chocolate cookie crumbs in between layers of white chocolate cheesecake batter to create cheesecake with a wavy black-and-white pattern.

Living on what she earns at the grief center combined with Charlie's pension makes Rose a little more frugal than your average transplanted widow. You might even say she's fricking frugal. Baking cheesecake is a way for Rose to save a few bucks, as she did when she created her own version of a chocolate and macadamia nut cheesecake after suffering sticker shock from a store-bought version. Whatever the source of her inspiration, Rose's cheesecakes are a welcome addition to her new roommates' all-night chat sessions and a favorite of her neighbors, with the exception of Frieda Claxton. For her, Rose makes Danish.

The Fall of St. Olaf
Pumpkin Cheesecake

MAKES 16 SERVINGS

Unlike Rose's painting *The Fall of St. Olaf*, this cheesecake *has* happened. Rose missed the crisp autumn weather in her hometown and the richer, heartier food that went along with it. So she put on a cozy goose sweater and whipped up this spice-scented creamy pumpkin cheesecake. The warm spices here are on the subtle side (unlike Rose's goose sweater). If you're a fan of intense pumpkin pie spices, up the quantities anywhere from a little bit all the way to double. A dollop of whipped cream topped with very thinly sliced candied ginger would be nice on slices of the finished cake. Really nice.

Gingersnap Cookie Crust (page 21), baked

1¼ cups pumpkin puree (puree, not "pie filling")

¼ cup maple syrup

2 teaspoons vanilla extract

¾ teaspoon ground cinnamon

½ teaspoon ground nutmeg

½ teaspoon ground ginger

½ teaspoon salt

2 pounds cream cheese, at room temperature

¾ cup granulated sugar

3 tablespoons cornstarch

4 large eggs, at room temperature

Options:

* Dollop some lightly whipped cream over each slice.

* Go one step further and top the cream with very thinly sliced candied ginger.

Heat the oven to 350°F with a rack in the center position. Prepare the springform pan for a water bath as described on page 38 and put it in a roasting pan. Keep a kettle of water hot over low heat.

Whisk the pumpkin puree, maple syrup, vanilla, cinnamon, nutmeg, ginger, and salt together in a bowl until the spices are well blended into the pumpkin. Using a handheld or stand mixer with the paddle attachment, beat the cream cheese, sugar, and cornstarch together in a separate bowl just until creamy and lump-free, stopping a few times to scrape down the bowl. Beat in the eggs one at a time, stopping to scrape down the bowl about halfway through. Switch to a whisk and stir in the pumpkin mix until thoroughly blended. Scrape down the bowl to make sure the batter is thoroughly blended.

Scrape the batter into the pan and wiggle the pan gently to even out the top. Pull out the oven rack, put the roasting pan on the rack, and pour in enough hot water to reach about 1 inch up the sides of the cake pan. Carefully slide the rack back in. Immediately lower the oven temperature to 300°F. Bake until about 3 inches around the edges of the cake are firm and the center is slightly jiggly, 60 to 70 minutes. (Don't check until at least 50 minutes into the baking.) Turn off the oven and leave the door slightly ajar. Cool, chill, and serve the cake according to the Tips on page 36.

White Chocolate Zebra Cheesecake

MAKES 16 SERVINGS

Rose, always the animal lover, prepares a cheesecake with layers of dark cookies and pale white cheesecake mix that make a lovely zebra pattern. Work patiently with the layering process and you'll be rewarded with a wavy black-and-white reveal in every slice. The bright red of the optional raspberry whipped cream makes a striking finishing touch.

Chocolate Cookie Crust (page 19); half for bottom the of the pan and other half for "zebra" layers

Softened butter for the pan

½ cup heavy cream

7 ounces very good-quality white chocolate, coarsely chopped (about 1⅓ cups)

1½ pounds cream cheese, at room temperature

½ cup sugar

4 teaspoons cornstarch

½ teaspoon salt

3 large eggs plus 1 egg yolk, at room temperature

1½ teaspoons vanilla extract

Heat the oven to 350°F with a rack in the center position. Make the chocolate cookie crust. Set aside half the mixture and use the remaining mix to line the bottom only of a 9-inch springform pan as described on page 15. Bake the crust 8 minutes and cool while making the batter.

Butter the sides of the springform pan. Prepare the pan for a water bath as described on page 38 and put it in a roasting pan. Keep a kettle of water hot over low heat.

Heat the heavy cream in a small saucepan just until bubbles form around the edges. Pour the hot cream over the white chocolate in a small heatproof bowl. Let stand 1 minute, then whisk gently just until completely free of lumps. Keep the white chocolate mixture warm while making the batter.

Using a handheld mixer or stand mixer with the paddle attachment, beat the cream cheese, sugar, cornstarch, and salt together on medium-low speed just until creamy and lump-free, stopping a few times to scrape down the bowl. Change the speed to low and beat in the eggs and yolk, one at a time, stopping about halfway through to scrape down the bowl. Check the melted white chocolate; it should still be warm and completely free of lumps. If not, rewarm over hot water, whisking constantly, just until creamy. Don't overheat or the white chocolate will separate. Switch to a whisk and beat the warm white chocolate mixture into the batter, making sure the mixture is free of lumps. Stir in the vanilla.

Spoon one-third of the batter over the crust and wiggle the pan to even out the layer. Sprinkle with half the reserved crust mix, making sure the crumbs come up to the sides of the pan (so you

(continued on page 81)

(continued from page 79)

can see them after baking). Gently spoon—don't pour—half the remaining batter over the crumbs. Nudge the batter with the back of the spoon into an even layer that reaches to the sides of the pan without disturbing the cookie crumbs. Top with the remaining crust mix and the remaining batter, again spooning the batter gently over the crumbs. Pull out the oven rack, put the roasting pan on the rack, and pour in enough hot water to reach about 1 inch up the sides of the cake pan. Carefully slide the rack back in. Immediately lower the oven temperature to 300°F. Bake until about 3 inches around the edges of the cake are firm and the center is slightly jiggly, about 1 hour and 10 minutes. (Don't check until at least 50 minutes into the baking.) Turn off the oven and leave the door slightly ajar. Cool, chill, and serve according to the Tips on page 36.

Options:

❋ Prepare the Crushed Raspberry Whipped Cream (page 28) and spoon a dollop over each serving.

❋ Decorate the top of the cheesecake with a circle of raspberries around the edge, pressing them gently into the cake. Sprinkle the raspberries with confectioners' sugar just before slicing and serving.

ROSE: *I think it's impossible to paint autumn in St. Olaf.*

DOROTHY: *How come?*

ROSE: *Maybe it's because of the horrible St. Olaf falling leaf story.*

DOROTHY: *Please, Rose. If this is a story about a man named Leif, I don't want to hear it.*

ROSE: *It's not that long.*

DOROTHY: *No.*

ROSE: *It has a surprise ending.*

DOROTHY: *All right, Rose. Just the ending, but keep it short.*

ROSE: *...*

ROSE: *Splat!*

Sunshine Cadet No-Bake Cheesecake Cupcakes

MAKES 10 CUPCAKES

In every crowd of Sunshine Cadets, there will be one cadet who's not afraid to kidnap a stuffed teddy bear and hold him hostage. While she and the bear are holed up waiting for ransom, the rest of the felony-free cadets can enjoy these no-bake cupcakes loaded with chocolaty-creamy goodness. These are perfect for a kid's birthday party or a just-got-out-of-jail celebration.

21 chocolate sandwich cookies

¾ cup chilled heavy cream

8 ounces cream cheese, at room temperature

2 tablespoons sugar

1½ teaspoons vanilla extract

Large pinch salt

Put sturdy cupcake liners (see note in Limoncello Cupcakes recipe, page 142) into ten cups of a twelve-cup muffin tin. Set aside.

With a rolling pin or wine bottle, crush 8 of the cookies between two sheets of parchment or wax paper. Roll until crushed however coarsely or finely you like. (A mix of very fine crumbs and small chunks is nice.) Move the crushed cookies to a bowl. Repeat with 8 more of the cookies. Scrape the cookie cream from the paper, add to the crushed cookies, and set the bowl aside. Using a hand-held mixer, beat the heavy cream in a small chilled bowl until the cream holds stiff peaks, but be careful not to overbeat. Keep cold while making the rest of the mixture.

Using a handheld mixer or stand mixer with the paddle attachment, beat the cream cheese, sugar, vanilla, and salt together (no need to clean the beaters if using a handheld mixer) on medium speed until fluffy, stopping a few times to scrape down the bowl. Using a rubber spatula, stir in the crushed cookies. Fold one-fourth of the whipped cream into the cream cheese mixture to lighten it, then fold in the rest of the cream just until there is no trace of unmixed whipped cream.

Spoon the mixture into the cups, dividing it evenly and pressing and scrunching it around gently with the back of the spoon so it fills out the sides and bottom of the liners. Leave the cupcakes with a rustic look or use the back of a teaspoon dipped in water to smooth the mixture so it resembles an iced cupcake. Cut the remaining 5 cookies into quarters and decorate the tops of the cupcakes with them however you like. Chill the cupcakes for at least 4 hours and up to overnight. Serve the cupcakes right out of the liners. (That's why you need sturdy liners!)

Cheese-Flan-Cake-Thingy

HALF FLAN, HALF CHEESECAKE

MAKES ONE 9-INCH FLAN, ABOUT 12 SERVINGS

Back in St. Olaf, Rose somehow mixed up her recipe for flan with her recipe for cheesecake. Sounds like something her neighbor Salvador would do. But like Salvador and his linguini with ear salve, the result of this happy mistake turned out to be quite delicious—a lovely, custardy cheesecake with a bittersweet caramel glaze.

FOR THE CARAMEL:

¾ cup sugar

FOR THE CUSTARD:

8 ounces cream cheese, at
  room temperature

⅓ cup sugar

¼ teaspoon salt

2 eggs plus 3 yolks

¼ cup sour cream

2½ teaspoons vanilla
  extract

1 cup milk

Get set up: Choose a wide heavy pan for the caramel. Have a 9-inch (measured across the bottom) glass pie pan, pot holders or oven mitts, and a roasting pan for the water bath nearby. Keep a kettle of water hot over low heat.

Make the caramel: Pour ¾ cup sugar into the pan and shake the pan to make an even layer. Put the pan over medium-low heat and watch. In 2 to 2½ minutes, the sugar will start to stick to the bottom of the pan and the sugar around the edges will start to liquefy. If the sugar takes longer than this to stick/liquefy, raise the heat slightly; less than this, lower the heat. Shake the pan to cover the liquid sugar with dry sugar. (Even in the best pans, the sugar will most likely liquefy unevenly.) The liquid sugar will start to color; continue shaking the pan as needed until all the sugar is liquefied and the color of a nice shiny penny. (You will want to stir the sugar as it liquefies and takes on color. Don't! It will crystallize, and you'll need to start again.) Immediately remove the pan from the heat and pour the caramel into the pie pan. Holding the pan by the top edges with pot holders or oven mitts, quickly and carefully tilt the pan to cover the bottom with caramel. The caramel must be used to line the pan immediately when it's ready; it will quickly become too firm to pour. Put the flan pan in the roasting pan. Making the caramel and lining the pan can be done up to 8 hours in advance.

Heat the oven to 325°F with a rack in the center position. Make the custard: Using a handheld mixer or a stand mixer with the paddle attachment, beat the cream cheese, sugar, and salt just until creamy and lump-free, stopping a few times to scrape down the bowl. Add the eggs and yolks gradually, stopping once or twice to scrape down

(continued on page 86)

(continued from page 84)

the bowl. Mix for a few seconds more. Switch to a whisk and whisk in the sour cream and vanilla, and then the milk. Scrape down the bowl and stir for a minute to make sure the batter is fully blended.

Pour the custard into the caramel-lined pan. Pull out the oven rack, put the roasting pan on the rack, and pour in enough hot water to reach halfway up the sides of the pie pan. Carefully slide the rack back in. Bake until the center of the flan is just a little wiggly, about 50 minutes. The flan may look undercooked, but it will set completely before cooling. Carefully lift the roasting pan out of the oven (no need to cool in the oven) and cool the flan in the water bath until the flan pan is cool enough to handle. Move the flan to a cooling rack to cool completely. Chill at least 6 hours, but preferably overnight.

To serve, place a large serving dish over the flan and quickly invert. Wait a few seconds for the flan to drop onto the plate. If it doesn't drop, wiggle the pie pan gently until it does. Some of the caramel will most likely be too firm to drip over the flan, but use a rubber spatula to scrape the liquid caramel that's still in the pan over the flan. Cut the chilled flan into wedges and serve chilled.

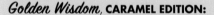

Golden Wisdom, CARAMEL EDITION:

- Choose a roasting/baking pan that is large enough to fit the pie pan but also fairly light, since you'll be lifting the hot pan with water and flan out of the oven. And make sure you have a landing place for the pan before you remove it from the oven.

- How to clean the pan after making caramel? Fill the pan with very hot water and walk away. In about half an hour, the caramel will be almost completely dissolved. Run a little hot water over the rest and then clean as usual.

- Caramel is a little tricky and is VERY hot when it reaches the right color. Be careful to use pot holders or oven mitts when working with the pan for caramel, and when tilting the pie pan to cover the bottom with caramel, hold the pan by only the rim. Do not attempt to hold the bottom of the pan.

Chocolate Macadamia Nut Cheesecake

MAKES 16 SERVINGS

Whether a cheesecake is needed for a talkfest or festive occasion, this elegant beauty fits the bill. Glazed with ganache, studded with toasted macadamia nuts, and sprinkled with more macadamia nuts, it makes quite a dramatic entrance.

4 ounces macadamia nuts (about 1 cup)

Baked Sugar Cookie Crust (page 22), made with some of the chopped toasted macadamia nuts (see step 1)

1½ pounds cream cheese, at room temperature

⅔ cup sugar

⅓ cup cocoa

1 tablespoon cornstarch

¼ teaspoon salt

3 large eggs, at room temperature

¼ cup sour cream

2 teaspoons vanilla extract

Ganache (page 27)

Heat the oven to 350°F with a rack in the center position. Spread the macadamia nuts out on a baking sheet and toast until golden brown, about 10 minutes. Cool to room temperature. Set aside 16 of the nicest whole nuts for decoration. Pulse the remaining nuts in a food processor in *very* short bursts until finely chopped. Don't overprocess or the nuts will turn oily.

Make the cookie crust, tossing ¼ cup of the chopped macadamia nuts with the flour before adding the flour to the butter. Line the bottom of a 9-inch springform pan with the nut crust as described on page 15 and bake. Let cool while making the cake.

Ensure the oven is at 350°F with a rack in the center position. Prepare the pan for a water bath as described on page 38 and put it in a roasting pan. Keep a kettle of water hot over low heat.

Using a handheld mixer or stand mixer with the paddle attachment, beat the cream cheese, sugar, cocoa, cornstarch, and salt together on medium-low speed just until creamy and lump-free, stopping a few times to scrape down the bowl. Beat in the eggs one at a time, stopping to scrape down the bowl about halfway through. Add the sour cream and vanilla and beat at low speed just until blended. Fold in ½ cup of the chopped toasted macadamia nuts and set the remaining nuts aside. Scrape down the bowl and make sure the batter is evenly mixed.

Scrape the batter into the crust and gently wiggle the pan to even out the top. Pull out the oven rack, put the roasting pan on the rack, and pour in enough hot water to reach about 1 inch up the sides of the cake pan. Carefully slide the rack back in. Immediately lower the

(continued on next page)

(continued from previous page)

oven temperature to 300°F. Bake until 2 inches of the cake around the edges is set and just the center is jiggly, about 1 hour. (Don't check until at least 50 minutes into the baking.) Turn off the oven and leave the door slightly ajar. Cool and chill the cake according to the Tips on page 36.

Set a cooling rack over a baking pan and set the cake on the rack. Make the ganache and, while it is still warm, pour it over the center of the cake so it runs to the edges and down the sides in thick drips. If you need to, nudge the ganache closer to the edges with the back of a spoon. Arrange the reserved whole macadamia nuts around the edge of the cake and scatter the remaining chopped nuts over the top. Serve right away or refrigerate for several hours before serving.

Golden Wisdom: Macadamia nuts are very high in oil, so they will start to brown quickly. Keep an eye on them after 5 minutes to make sure they don't burn.

DOROTHY: *Rose, what are you doing out? I thought you were asleep.*

ROSE: *I went out to get provisions. I figured we'd be up all night talking.*

DOROTHY: *Eh, I'm going to bed.*

BLANCHE: *She don't feel like talking.*

ROSE: *But I got chocolate macadamia nut cheesecake and rum raisin ice cream.*

DOROTHY: *Oh, all right. Start cutting. You scoop.*

Brownie-Cheesecake Bars

MAKES SIXTEEN 2 X 2-INCH BARS, BUT BE A REBEL LIKE ROSE AND CUT THEM ANY WAY YOU LIKE

No wonder these are a favorite of Rose's—mixing and swirling the batters together is like finger painting. Rose isn't the only one who adores these. Uncle Hingeblotter was known to burn through a tray of these in a single sitting. Or maybe Baby helped?

**FOR THE BROWNIES
(or use a brownie mix;
see note on next page):**

8 ounces good-quality semisweet chocolate (about 70%)

6 tablespoons unsalted butter, plus more for the pan

½ cup all-purpose flour, plus more for the pan

1 teaspoon baking powder

¼ teaspoon fine salt

¼ cup sugar

2 large eggs, at room temperature

1 tablespoon vanilla extract

FOR THE CHEESECAKE SWIRL-IN:

8 ounces cream cheese, at room temperature

¼ cup sugar

¼ teaspoon salt

1 egg, at room temperature

½ teaspoon vanilla extract

¼ cup sour cream

Make the brownies: Melt the chocolate and butter in the top of a double boiler (see Golden Wisdom following the Double Fudge Chocolate Cheesecake on page 52) over low heat. Stir occasionally until the chocolate is melted and the mixture is smooth, about 10 minutes. Or melt the chocolate and butter in a microwave oven using short bursts and stirring between each burst. Either way, use low heat so the chocolate doesn't stick and scald. Let cool to room temperature.

Heat the oven to 325°F with a rack in the center position. Lightly butter and flour a 9 × 9-inch baking pan. If you like, prepare parchment paper handles as described in Blanche's Fortieth Birthday Cheesecake Squares recipe on page 106.

Sift the flour, baking powder, and salt into a bowl and set aside. Beat the sugar, eggs, and vanilla in a separate bowl on medium speed just until foamy. Beat this mixture into the chocolate mixture until smooth. Fold in the flour just until no streaks of white remain. Pour the batter into the pan and smooth into an even layer. Set aside.

Make the cheesecake swirl-in: Using a hand mixer, beat the cream cheese, sugar, and salt together in a bowl just until creamy and lump-free. Scrape down the bowl, beat in the egg and vanilla, and scrape the bowl again. Beat in the sour cream at low speed just until blended. Scrape the bowl well to make sure everything is well mixed.

Make an even layer of cheesecake batter over the brownie batter. Using a serving spoon and starting at one edge, bring the side of the spoon straight down to the bottom of the pan, then turn and lift the spoon to bring some of the brownie batter up through the cheesecake batter to make a swirl. Use a small rubber spatula or your finger to wipe any batter off the spoon in between swirls. Make the swirl as chunky or feathered as you like. Wiggle the pan vigorously to settle

(continued on next page)

(continued from previous page)

the batter, though not as vigorously as Blanche shook Rose when she found out Rose ate her sensible meal and drank her shake.

Bake until the edges are set, about 25 minutes. A cake tester or wooden pick inserted into the middle of the brownies will come out gooey. Crack the oven door open a bit and let the pan sit in the oven 30 minutes. Cool completely on a rack before refrigerating. Chill at least 6 hours or, better yet, overnight. Cut into squares or bars and serve.

Golden Wisdom: Any boxed mix that makes a 9 x 9-inch cake pan of brownies can be substituted for the brownie portion of this recipe.

ROSE *[discussing her paintings]: I call them* Winter of St. Olaf, *and* Spring of St. Olaf, *and* Summer of St. Olaf.

DONALD: *Why haven't you painted* The Fall of St. Olaf?

ROSE: *Because it hasn't happened yet. Although we came pretty close when New Math came along.*

COCKTAILS WITH

Rose

Ginger-Orange Syrup

MAKES ABOUT 3 CUPS

Rose was known around St. Olaf for her preserves. Preserving is not so easy to do in Miami, what with her work at the grief center, Spanish lessons, weekends away with Ernie, and all the rest. Rose still likes the thought of putting something by, so having a jar of ginger-orange syrup or rosemary-infused pear nectar in the fridge is right up her alley. You can take the girl out of St. Olaf . . .

2 oranges

12 slices peeled ginger the thickness of a quarter

3 cups water

½ cup sugar

Use a vegetable peeler to remove the zest from the oranges in wide strips, avoiding the white pith underneath. Drop the strips of zest and the ginger into a 1-quart mason or other heatproof jar. Squeeze the juice from the oranges into the jar. Heat the water and sugar in a small saucepan, stirring just until the sugar is dissolved. Pour directly over the zest and ginger. Let sit until cooled to room temperature. Cover and let stand for at least 4 hours and up to overnight before using. Refrigerate until needed. The refrigerated syrup will last at least 2 weeks, but remove the orange zest after about 4 days.

GINGER-ORANGE SPRITZER: Fill a tall glass with ice, pour in ¼ to ⅓ cup of the syrup, and top off with club soda or sparkling water.

GINGER-ORANGE COCKTAIL TIPS: Add some white rum, gin, or vodka to the above spritzer. Replace simple syrup with ginger-orange syrup in cocktails that would benefit from a little kick, like Dorothy's New Fashioned. Or add a little to a shaker full of orangey drinks, like Dorothy's Gold Coast Cosmo or Sophia's Harvey Wallbanger.

Rosemary-Infused Pear Nectar (With or Without Vodka)

MAKES ABOUT 3 CUPS, ENOUGH FOR 9 TO 12 DRINKS

Most people don't think of pairing herbs with fruit, and that's a shame. Basil, for example, marries beautifully with orange in the Mel Bushman (page 123). Here rosemary makes a wonderful addition to pear juice rounded out with a little sugar and a little lemon juice. The result is delicious in a cocktail or mocktail.

½ cup Simple Syrup (page 40)

2 big sprigs of rosemary

3 cups pear juice

¼ cup lemon juice

If making the simple syrup, add 1 sprig of rosemary just before removing it from the heat. If you have syrup on hand, heat ½ cup of it until steaming, then drop in one sprig of rosemary. Cool the syrup to room temperature. Don't leave the rosemary in the syrup much longer than that or the syrup will turn bitter. Pull out the rosemary sprig and pour the syrup into a 1-quart mason or other type of jar. Add the remaining sprig of rosemary, the pear juice, and the lemon juice. Screw on the top of the jar, shake well, and store in the refrigerator for at least 1 day before using and up to 1 week.

Rosemary-Pear Martini

MAKES 1 MARTINI (CAN SCALE UP AS NEEDED)

2 ounces (¼ cup) Rosemary-Infused Pear Nectar (above)

1½ ounces (3 tablespoons) vodka of your choice

Wedge of lemon

Rosemary sprig and/or ½ lemon slice for garnish, optional

Fill a small cocktail shaker two-thirds full of ice. Pour the pear nectar and vodka over the ice. Squeeze in the lemon. Cap the shaker and shake vigorously until the outside of the shaker is frosty. Strain into a coupe or small martini glass. Garnish with a sprig of rosemary and/or lemon slice if you like.

ROSEMARY-PEAR SPRITZER: For a vodka-less mocktail, fill a tall glass with ice. Fill halfway with the pear nectar (¼ to ⅓ cup) and add an equal amount of club soda or sparkling water. (Or find the proportions that work for you.) Drop or squeeze in a lemon wedge.

Muddled Cucumber Gin and Tonic (or Ginless Tonic)

MAKES 1 DRINK

Finding a muddled drink in Rose's chapter is no coincidence. Muddled is, after all, how Rose spends most of her days. Cucumber and gin make good buddies, one complementing the other. If gin and tonics say summer, then gin and tonics (or just plain tonics) muddled with cucumber say summer in an English garden.

3 thick slices English cucumber

1 lime wedge

Tiny pinch salt

1½ ounces (3 tablespoons) gin, optional

Tonic water

Cucumber ribbons (see note) or slices, or lime wedges for garnish

Muddle the cucumber, lime, and salt in a tall glass until the cucumber and lime are well bruised. Add the gin, if using, and enough ice to fill the glass. Pour in the tonic water, give the drink a stir, and garnish.

Note: To make cucumber ribbons, use a vegetable peeler to remove a long strip of peel from a medium cucumber. Discard this strip. Continue removing ribbons with the peeler until you reach the seeds. Turn the cuke around and do the same to the other side. Curl the ribbons around a long wooden pick, or just curl the ribbons, and tuck the curls into the drink to let them unfurl.

ROSE: *Tell me, is it possible to love two men at the same time?*

BLANCHE: *Set the scene. Have we been drinking?*

Spiked Hot Milk Chocolate

MAKES 2 MUGFULS

Most women's fantasy romance features tall flutes filled with sparkling champagne. In Rose's fantasy, the beverage of choice is rich hot chocolate with, of course, mini marshmallows. And a glug of something, if you like.

½ cup half-and-half, regular or fat-free (see note)

6 ounces good-quality milk chocolate (52 percent, if possible)

Large pinch salt

2 cups milk

2 ounces (¼ cup) spirit of your choice, such as coffee liqueur, grappa, hazelnut liqueur, or orange liqueur, optional

Mini marshmallows

Note: If you'd like to skip the half-and-half, use another ½ cup of milk in its place.

Heat the half-and-half, milk chocolate, and salt together in a small heavy saucepan over low heat. Using a rubber spatula, stir occasionally until the chocolate is melted. Pour in the milk in a thin steady stream and continue stirring until the milk is steaming and bubbles form around the edge of the saucepan. Pour into 2 hot mugs and stir in the liqueur, if using. Top with mini marshmallows.

ROSE: *If I ever got another chance at a second Mr. Right, I'd want somebody entirely different from Charlie . . . I'd like somebody really wild. Somebody impulsive, who'd sweep me off my feet. He'd pick me up in his convertible Porsche and whisk me to the airport. And we'd fly to his villa in the south of France, where we'd blindfold the orchestra and dance until dawn. And then we'd watch the sun come up over two steaming cups of cocoa.*

SOPHIA: *Cocoa?*

ROSE: *With little marshmallows.*

Stinking Hot Toddies

MAKES 1 TODDY

Got the flu? Stuck in a house with two other people just as sick and bitchy as you? No wise old Sicilian woman to take care of you and offer traditional cures? Drag yourself to the liquor cabinet and then to the kitchen, armed with this recipe and a mug. Your disposition will be headed toward cheerful shortly.

1½ ounces (3 tablespoons) bourbon, rye, or Canadian whiskey

1 to 1½ ounces (2 to 3 tablespoons) lemon juice

1 ounce (2 tablespoons) honey

¾ to 1 cup boiling water

OPTIONAL BUT NICE:
Lemon slice
Cinnamon stick
A few whole cloves

Put the whiskey, lemon juice, and honey in a mug. Add whichever optional ingredients you like. Pour the boiling water into the mug and let steep just until cool enough to drink, but still hot. Lie back on the couch, throw a blanket over yourself, and enjoy.

Option: Make a virgin toddy as described above, leaving out the whiskey. The more optional but nice ingredients that go into a virgin toddy, the better.

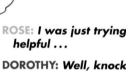

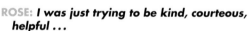

ROSE: *I was just trying to be kind, courteous, helpful . . .*

DOROTHY: *Well, knock it off! I've had it up to here with your cheerful disposition.*

ROSE: *Oh, do you think it's easy to be cheerful around you two? You know how many of these stinking hot toddies I have to drink to keep on a happy face?*

Rose-Colored Lemonade

MAKES 5 TO 6 TALL GLASSES OF LEMONADE

Steeping mashed raspberries in sugar syrup lends the finished lemonade a beautiful rosy tint as well as a subtly delicious hint of the berries.

One half-pint basket fresh raspberries

1 cup Simple Syrup (page 40)

½ cup freshly squeezed lemon juice

Still water, club soda, or sparkling water as needed, about ½ cup per serving

Mash about half the raspberries in a small bowl. Pour in the simple syrup and let stand at room temperature 1 to 2 hours. Strain into a small glass pitcher and discard the mashed raspberries. Stir in the lemon juice and refrigerate until well chilled, at least 4 hours and up to 2 days.

To serve: Fill a tall glass with ice. Pour in ¼ to $^1/_3$ cup of the lemon juice mix. Top up the glass with still or sparkling water. Serve very cold, adding a few raspberries to each glass if you like.

BLANCHE: *Let me get the cheesecake and we'll talk. . . . (gasps) Oh my god!*
DOROTHY: *Blanche, what's wrong?*
BLANCHE: *Here we are in the middle of a crisis and there's no cheesecake!*

Blanche

ONCE UPON A Southern time in Georgia: A hot-to-trot Atlanta widow gives up life as a belle and buys a house in Miami. Her plan? To cover the mortgage (with a 7 percent interest rate from Miami Federal) on her new home by renting out rooms to other single women her age. While the plan may not have gone exactly as expected, she does find two women to share her home. The fourth woman is pure gravy. Or more like a rich, spicy marinara sauce.

That Southern belle was Blanche Devereaux, and those three women—Rose, Dorothy, and Sophia—became much more than tenants: they became her family. When Blanche is feeling lower than the rent on a burning building, they are there for her. Sophia imparts the wisdom of her old age, Dorothy dispenses practical advice, and Rose, well . . . Rose does whatever is it that she does.

Blanche isn't much of a baker, but she sure is a great dater. If the way to a man's heart is through his stomach, it would be in Blanche's best interest to pick up a trick or two. (In the kitchen, of course.) After all, suppose there's a sudden run on smoked oysters and Cold Duck, or Marguerite leaves before finishing her latest batch of aphrodisiac? Blanche needs to be prepared for anything, and that may even mean learning to bake.

We may never know which of Blanche's sisters patiently taught her how to create a luscious cheesecake dripping with pecan pie goodness (however, all signs point to Virginia), or what she did to wheedle Fidel Santiago's cheesecake recipe from him. But we can be sure that whatever sacrifices Blanche has made along the way come under the heading of "All's fair in love and war."

Blanche's Fortieth Birthday Cheesecake Squares

MAKES SIXTEEN 2 X 2-INCH BARS

Dirk called his mom for this recipe and made these festive squares for Blanche on her fortieth birthday. (Dirk had a watercress salad with two lemon wedges.) Next year, Jake from VIP Catering made them for her fortieth birthday. A year later, when Mel Bushman offered to bake a batch to celebrate her fortieth, Blanche said, "Enough with the birthday cheesecake squares, already! I mean, how many times can a girl turn forty?!"

Adding a dollop of whipped cream and more sprinkles would be festive. Inviting Mr. Ha Ha and a bunch of kids over to sing "Happy Birthday" would be totally over the top.

½ **recipe Graham Cracker Crust (page 18)**

Softened butter for the pan

1 egg plus 1 yolk

¼ **cup sour cream**

¼ **cup milk (preferably whole)**

4 teaspoons vanilla extract

1 pound cream cheese, at room temperature

⅓ **cup sugar**

4 tablespoons unsalted butter, at room temperature

2 teaspoons cornstarch

¼ **teaspoon salt**

4 tablespoons sprinkles of your choice

½ **cup chilled heavy cream, optional**

Additional sprinkles for decorating, optional

Heat the oven to 350°F with a rack in the center position. Butter the sides of an 8-inch square cake pan (even if it's nonstick). Cut a piece of parchment paper wide enough to barely fit the width of the pan and long enough to come up the sides at least to the top edge of the pan. The parchment will come in handy when lifting the cake squares out.

Make ½ recipe of graham cracker crust. Be sure the parchment paper is in place (crease the paper so it fits neatly into the corners of the pan). Using a small glass with a flat bottom covered in plastic wrap, tamp the crust into the prepared pan so it covers the bottom evenly. Tamp down the corners with a spoon or your fingers. Bake the crust for 10 minutes and cool while making the batter.

Adjust the oven to 325°F. Stir together the egg and yolk, sour cream, milk, and vanilla extract in a small bowl and set aside. Using a handheld or stand mixer with the paddle attachment, beat the cream cheese, sugar, 4 tablespoons butter, cornstarch, and salt on medium-low speed just until creamy and lump-free, stopping to scrape down the bowl twice. Beat in the egg mixture on low speed just until blended, stopping to scrape down the bowl once or twice. Use the rubber spatula to stir in 3 tablespoons of the sprinkles by hand. Scrape the batter into the pan and sprinkle the remaining 1 tablespoon of sprinkles over the top.

(continued on page 108)

(continued from page 106)

Bake until the edges are set and the center is slightly jiggly, about 25 minutes. Turn off the oven, open the door all the way, and leave the cake in the oven until the oven is completely cool, about 30 minutes. Cool and chill the cake according to the Tips on page 36.

To serve, free the sides of the cake with no parchment by running a very thin knife along them. Cut the cake into 2-inch squares (or whatever size and shape you like). Starting with the squares next to the parchment, move the squares onto a serving dish, using the parchment to help you lift the pieces a little and get them neatly onto the dish. For the optional topping, whip the heavy cream in a chilled bowl until it holds soft peaks. Dollop a little onto each square and top the dollop with a sprinkling of sprinkles.

BLANCHE: *I used to attract men who were young and active and virile, but now they just want to date girls in their twenties and thirties. What's a great-looking gal in her forties to do?*

DOROTHY: *Perhaps we should find one and ask her.*

Mocha Chocolata Yá! Yá! Cheesecake

MAKES 16 SERVINGS

Just the thought of sliding a fork into a slice of this cheesecake makes Blanche warm and tingly. Too warm and too tingly and too hot! Bake one and you'll understand why the blend of milk chocolate and coffee flavors has that effect on her.

Chocolate Cookie Crust (page 19) for bottom and sides of pan, baked

6 ounces milk chocolate (see note)

½ cup heavy cream

3 large eggs, at room temperature

2 tablespoons instant espresso

2 teaspoons vanilla extract

2 pounds cream cheese, at room temperature

1 cup sugar

2 tablespoons cornstarch

¼ teaspoon salt

Options:

* Bake the cake without the crust.

* Whip ½ cup chilled heavy cream until it holds firm peaks. Use a pastry bag with a star tip to decorate the edges of the cake with little stars of the whipped cream. Had a rough night at the Rusty Anchor last night? Skip the pastry bag and use a teaspoon to make 16 little dollops instead of the rosettes.

* Nestle chocolate-covered espresso beans in each dollop of whipped cream.

Heat the oven to 350°F with a rack in the center position. Prepare the pan for a water bath as described on page 38 and put it in a roasting pan. Keep a kettle of water hot over low heat.

Heat the chocolate and heavy cream in a small heavy saucepan over very low heat, whisking occasionally, until the chocolate is completely melted and blended into the heavy cream. Remove from the heat but leave in the warm pan while making the batter. Lightly beat the eggs, instant espresso, and vanilla together in a small bowl and set aside. Don't worry if the espresso forms little clumps.

Using a handheld or stand mixer with the paddle attachment, beat together the cream cheese, sugar, cornstarch, and salt on medium-low speed just until creamy and lump-free. Stop once or twice to scrape down the bowl. Add the egg mixture and beat at low speed, stopping once or twice to scrape down the bowl, until no streaks are left. Switch to a whisk and stir in the chocolate mixture by hand.

Pour the batter into the crust and gently wiggle the pan to even out the top. Pull out the oven rack, put the roasting pan on the rack, and pour in enough hot water to reach about 1 inch up the sides of the cake pan. Carefully slide the rack back in. Immediately lower the oven temperature to 300°F. Bake until about 2 inches around the edges of the cake are firm and the center is slightly jiggly, about 1 hour and 15 minutes. (Don't check until at least 1 hour into the baking.) Turn off the oven and leave the door slightly ajar. Cool, chill, and serve according to the Tips on page 36.

Note: Milk chocolate with a higher cocoa percentage, around 55%, is perfect for this cake. If you can't find that, any high-quality milk chocolate will work beautifully.

Guava Cheesecake at Midnight

MAKES 16 SERVINGS

When Blanche made plans with Fidel Santiago for "dessert at midnight," could this be what he had in mind? As any Cuban dessert baker can tell you, sweetened condensed milk and guava are top-of-the-list pantry items. This dense, creamy, and not-too-sweet cheesecake has a generous topping made with guava paste.

Softened butter for the pan

1½ pounds cream cheese, at room temperature

½ cup sugar

4 teaspoons cornstarch

¼ teaspoon salt

4 large eggs, at room temperature

2 teaspoons vanilla extract

¾ cup sweetened condensed milk

½ cup sour cream

FOR THE GUAVA TOPPING: See page 29

Options:

* Make and bake a Vanilla Wafer Crust (page 20) for this cake.

* Create your own version of this masterpiece by replacing the guava topping with Dulce de Leche (page 26).

Heat the oven to 350°F with a rack in the center position. Butter a nonstick 9-inch springform pan. Prepare the pan for a water bath as described on page 38 and put it in a roasting pan. Keep a kettle of water hot over low heat.

Using a handheld mixer or stand mixer with the paddle attachment, beat the cream cheese, sugar, cornstarch, and salt together on medium-low speed just until creamy and lump-free, scraping down the bowl a few times. Beat in the eggs one by one, adding the vanilla with the first egg and scraping down the bowl halfway through. Switch to a whisk and stir in the condensed milk and sour cream by hand.

Scrape the batter into the pan and gently wiggle to even out the top. Pull out the oven rack, put the roasting pan on the rack, and pour in enough hot water to reach about 1 inch up the sides of the cake pan. Carefully slide the rack back in. Immediately lower the oven temperaturet to 300°F. Bake until about 2 inches around the edges of the cake are firm and the center is slightly jiggly, 60 to 70 minutes. (Don't check until at least 50 minutes into the baking.) Turn off the oven and leave the door slightly ajar. Cool and chill according to the Tips on page 36.

When the cake is chilled, make the topping. Spread the still-warm—*not hot!*—topping over the cheesecake and refrigerate again until the topping is set.

Pecan Pie, Meet Cheesecake. Cheesecake, This Is Pecan Pie

MAKES 16 SERVINGS

Can't choose between two of America's favorite desserts? Don't. Bake a creamy, rich cheesecake flavored with brown sugar and dark corn syrup—just like a pecan pie—and then top it with a flowy version of pecan pie filling.

Graham Cracker Crust (page 18) for the bottom and sides of the pan, baked

2 pounds cream cheese, at room temperature

½ cup light brown sugar

4 teaspoons cornstarch

½ teaspoon salt

3 large eggs, at room temperature

¼ cup dark corn syrup

1½ teaspoons vanilla extract

FOR THE TOPPING:

½ cup dark corn syrup

1 tablespoon butter

1 cup pecan pieces

2 tablespoons water

Options:

* Make a nutty crust by adding ¼ cup toasted pecan pieces to the graham crackers in the food processor.

* Add 1 tablespoon bourbon to the skillet along with the corn syrup and butter for a mellow touch of the old South.

Heat the oven to 350°F with a rack in the center position. Prepare the springform pan for a water bath as described on page 38 and put it in a roasting pan. Keep a kettle of water hot over low heat.

Using a handheld mixer or stand mixer with the paddle attachment, beat the cream cheese, brown sugar, cornstarch, and salt together on medium-low speed just until creamy and lump-free, stopping a few times to scrape down the sides of the bowl. Change the speed to low and beat in the eggs, adding them one at a time and stopping halfway through to scrape the bowl. With the mixer still on low, beat in ¼ cup corn syrup and vanilla just until blended. Scrape the bowl well and make sure the batter is thoroughly mixed.

Scrape the batter into the crust and gently wiggle the pan to even out the top. Pull out the oven rack, put the roasting pan on the rack, and pour in enough hot water to reach about 1 inch up the sides of the cake pan. Carefully slide the rack back in. Immediately lower the oven temperature to 300°F. Bake until about 2 inches around the edges of the cake are firm and the center is slightly jiggly, about 60 minutes. (Don't check until at least 45 minutes into the baking.) Turn off the oven and leave the door slightly ajar. Cool and chill according to the Tips on page 36.

While the cake is chilling, make the topping: Heat ½ cup corn syrup and the butter in a medium skillet over medium-low heat just until the butter is melted. Stir in the pecans and bring just to a simmer. Remove from the heat and stir in the water. Set aside to cool. Spoon the topping over the chilled cake and serve at room temperature (for a topping that's drippy in a good way) or refrigerate the topped cake (for a firmer topping).

Get It While It's Hot! Peach Upside-Down Cobbler-Cheesecake

MAKES 8 SERVINGS

Toss the peaches with the preserves and make the batter hours in advance and you've got yourself an almost completely do-ahead dessert. Think of this as a kind of peach cobbler, only with warm, creamy cheesecake topping. Delish.

Softened butter for the baking dish

4 ripe medium peaches, pitted and cut into 1-inch slices (about 3 cups) or a 16-ounce bag of frozen sliced peaches, defrosted and drained

¼ cup peach preserves, orange marmalade, or a mix of peach and raspberry preserves

12 ounces cream cheese, at room temperature

¼ cup sugar

¼ teaspoon salt

1 egg plus 1 yolk, at room temperature

¼ cup sour cream

1½ teaspoons vanilla extract

Butter an 8 × 8-inch baking dish or other baking dish of a similar size. Stir the peaches and preserves together in the baking dish. Let stand, stirring once or twice, until the preserves are loosened up enough to coat the peaches with a rich glaze. This much can be done up to several hours in advance. Cover with plastic wrap and leave at room temperature.

Heat the oven to 300°F with a rack in the center position. Using a handheld or stand mixer with the paddle attachment, beat the cream cheese, sugar, cornstarch, and salt together on medium-low speed just until creamy and lump-free. Beat in the egg and yolk, stopping once to scrape down the bowl. Stir in the sour cream and vanilla extract on low speed. The batter can be made up to 3 hours in advance and refrigerated.

Spoon the batter over the peaches to cover them evenly. If using refrigerated batter, dollop the batter over the peaches and let the batter warm up for 5 to 10 minutes before spreading. Bake until the edges are set and the center is slightly jiggly, 45 to 50 minutes. Some peach juices may bubble up around the edges. Turn off the oven, open the door halfway, and leave the baking dish in the oven for 30 minutes. Serve warm. Leftovers served chilled are nice, too.

Blanche's No-Bake Georgia Peanut Butter Cheesecake

MAKES 8 SERVINGS

A little *Golden Girls* math: Blanche = Georgia = peanuts. Blanche's life – time spent cooking = less time to date, hence this no-cook cheesecake. It's easy enough to cut the chocolate cookie crust recipe in half to use here, but you have two other options: Make the full amount of crust, double the recipe to make two cakes, and freeze one. Or freeze the unused half of the crust for the next time you make this cake. And there will be a next time.

½ **recipe Chocolate Cookie Crust (page 19)**

½ **cup heavy cream**

1 **tablespoons confectioners' sugar**

8 **ounces cream cheese, at room temperature**

1 **cup peanut butter**

½ **cup granulated sugar**

¼ **cup very coarsely chopped salted peanuts**

Make the half recipe of chocolate cookie crust and set 2 tablespoons aside. Press the remaining crust mix into the bottom only of a 9-inch springform pan (see page 15). Blanche strongly suggests using a parchment circle for this no-bake crust to make moving the cake from the pan to a cake stand or serving platter (not to mention cutting and serving) easier. Chill the crust while making the filling.

Using a handheld mixer, beat the heavy cream and confectioners' sugar in a small chilled bowl just until the cream holds stiff peaks. Be careful not to overbeat. Keep cold until needed. In a separate bowl (no need to clean the beaters), beat the cream cheese, peanut butter, and granulated sugar together until fluffy, stopping a few times to scrape down the bowl. Using a rubber spatula, fold one-fourth of the whipped cream into the peanut butter mixture to lighten it, then fold in the rest just until you can see no trace of whipped cream.

Scrape the filling over the crust. Smooth out the top while working the batter into the corners and against the sides of the pan. (An offset spatula works well for this.) Decorate the top with the reserved crust mix and chopped peanuts any way you like. (But remember, Blanche has a museum-trained eye for this kind of thing.) Refrigerate the cheesecake for at least 4 hours and up to overnight. Once the filling is set, at least 2 hours, run a thin-bladed knife around the edge of the pan, remove the sides of the pan, and cover the cheesecake with plastic wrap. Chill at least 2 hours and up to overnight before serving.

Many of Blanche's cocktails have a citrusy kick, keeping them fresh and very sippable. Could that preference have come from her stint as chair of the Citrus Festival Ball?

Here? So Close to Cuba?

BLANCHE'S TAKE ON A MOJITO

MAKES 2
(ONE FOR YOU AND ONE FOR YOUR GENTLEMAN CALLER)

It's almost as if Big Daddy went to Cuba on vacation and came back with a tropical take on his beloved mint julep (page 127), with rum replacing the bourbon and a squirt of lime juice because, well, Cuba.

16 fresh mint leaves, plus sprigs for garnish

2 sugar cubes or 4 teaspoons white sugar, or to taste

1 lime, cut into 8 wedges

3 ounces (about ⅓ cup) white rum

Club soda or sparkling water

Divide the mint leaves and sugar between 2 tall glasses. Drop 2 lime wedges into each glass. Muddle all together until the mint is torn into rough pieces and the sugar is dissolved. Stir half the rum into each glass, then fill with cracked ice. Fill the glasses with sparkling water and stir (see Golden Wisdom below). Float a lime wedge on top if you like.

Golden Wisdom: You know those long thin spoons that come with cocktail sets? There's a reason why the handle of the spoon has that unusual helix shape. The best and least messy way to mix a tall cocktail like this is to slip the spoon into the drink and roll the handle back and forth between your palms. Those little spiral grooves will mix from top to bottom without splashing or spilling

Slow Comfortable Screw

MAKES 2 DRINKS

Here's another delicious way to put to use that bottle of nice sloe gin you bought for the Dr. Elliot Clayton (page 124). The SCS is one of Blanche's favorites. 'Nuff said.

1 ounce vodka

1 ounce sloe gin

1 ounce Southern Comfort whiskey liqueur

Fresh orange juice, for floating

Orange cube or slice (page 44)

Fill a large cocktail shaker most of the way full of ice. Pour in the vodka, sloe gin, and Southern Comfort. Shake gently but thoroughly. Pour the drink along with the ice into 2 Old Fashioned glasses. Use a spoon to float the orange juice over the top of the drink, letting it settle slowly to the bottom. Add an orange cube or slice for garnish.

DOROTHY: *Blanche. Your picture's in the paper. And there's a big article about the Citrus Festival.*

BLANCHE: *What's it say, what's it say?*

DOROTHY: *"Miami will be busy this weekend with ten major conventions"—listen to this—"the highlight being the Citrus Festival Ball, which is being chaired this year by thirty-five-year-old Blanche Devereaux."*

DOROTHY: *How much did that cost you?*

BLANCHE: *I don't have to pay for my compliments.*

DOROTHY: *You went to bed with him?*

BLANCHE: *Twice. But it's not like I wouldn't have anyway.*

Hazelnut Alexander

MAKES 2 DRINKS

Very retro--the perfect cocktail to sip while watching an *I Love Lucy* marathon. Nutty, chocolaty, creamy. What's not to like?

2 ounces (¼ cup) hazelnut liqueur

2 ounces (¼ cup) crème de cacao

2 ounces (¼ cup) half-and-half, regular or fat free

1 whole nutmeg for grating, or ground nutmeg

Fill a large cocktail shaker two-thirds full of ice. Pour the hazelnut liqueur, crème de cacao, and half-and-half over the ice. Shake vigorously and strain into 2 coupes or small martini glasses. Grate a tiny bit of the whole nutmeg over the top or flick on a little ground nutmeg using the tip of a paring knife.

The Mel Bushman

MAKES 1 DRINK

As Blanche discovered when Mel Bushman went out of town without a heads-up, certain things that are taken for granted shouldn't be. Consider vermouth, sitting there all alone, waiting for someone to make a martini. Maybe it's time for vermouth to go from supporting role to headliner, as it does in this very simple cocktail bursting with herby-orangey goodness.

2 to 3 basil leaves

½ orange slice

Large pinch sugar

3 ounces (generous ⅓ cup) dry white vermouth

Muddle the basil leaves, orange, and sugar gently in a rocks or Old Fashioned glass. Fill the glass halfway with ice, pour in the vermouth, and give the drink a big stir.

MEL BUSHMAN: *I got a great idea. Why don't you come over to my place? I'm hungry. I'll go down to Wolfie's, get some pastrami. We can rent Out of Africa.*

BLANCHE: *We've rented it five times and never made it through to the end.*

MEL BUSHMAN: *I know, but it always works.*

The Dr. Elliot Clayton

SLOE GIN FIZZ WITH A KICK

MAKES 2 (ONE FOR YOU AND ONE FOR DR. CLAYTON)

Yuzu juice is some mad combination of a few citrusy flavors, mandarin, lemon, and very sweet grapefruit among them. If you find fresh yuzus, squeeze the juice for this delicious take on a classic Sloe Gin Fizz. If not, you may find yuzu juice, refrigerated or frozen, in well-stocked grocery stores. Or simply use the juice from your favorite citrus fruit. Spend a little on a quality sloe gin, avoiding the overly sweet, syrupy brands.

4 ounces (½ cup) sloe gin

1½ to 2 ounces (3 to 4 tablespoons) yuzu juice, lemon juice, lime juice, or any mix of citrus juices you prefer

Club soda or sparkling water

Lime or lemon slices, optional

Pour the sloe gin and yuzu juice over 6 hefty ice cubes in a cocktail shaker. Shake vigorously and pour into 2 rocks glasses, dividing the ice evenly. Pour in enough club soda to fill the glasses almost but not all the way to the top. Add a lime or lemon slice if you like and serve.

BLANCHE: *May I offer you a drink?*

DR. ELLIOT CLAYTON: *Why, sure, if you'll join me.*

BLANCHE: *I don't mind if I do. What would you like?*

ELLIOT: *Something smooth and sweet with a little kick to it.*

BLANCHE: *Hmm. How about a Sloe Gin Fizz?*

ELLIOT: *You're talking about the drink and I'm talking about the bartender.*

The Big Daddy

AKA THE MINT JULEP

MAKES 1 MINT JULEP

Bourbon seems a logical choice for Big Daddy to have stashed in his Bible. And from bourbon to julep is just a hop, skip, and a jump. No need to wait for Kentucky Derby Day to enjoy this; any ol' time will do. Serve the Big Daddy alongside boiled peanuts or thin pimento cheese sandwiches on white bread to get that full Southern vibe going.

1 to 2 teaspoons sugar, preferably superfine

6 mint leaves

1½ ounces (3 tablespoons) Kentucky bourbon

Muddle the sugar and mint in a rocks or Old Fashioned glass until the mint leaves are very bruised. Pour in the bourbon and fill the glass halfway with ice. Give a big stir and serve.

BLANCHE: *Daddy!*

BIG DADDY: *Baby girl! Looking at you takes my breath away! Hair as shiny as the dew on a field of sunflowers, eyes that sparkle bluer than the Mississippi, and the prettiest smile on either side of the Mason-Dixon Line!*

BLANCHE: *Didn't I tell you my daddy was the smartest man who ever lived?*

Sophia

PICTURE IT: MIAMI, 2092. As she predicted, a cranky old woman outlives her housemates by decades. She takes ownership of the home they shared, she finds new roommates, and they all live with the assistance of the many cloned Cocos, known affectionately as "the Coco-ettes." Just about every morning finds her whipping up cheesecakes made with creamy ricotta, rich chocolate, fresh eggs, nutty-sweet amaretto—oh, hell, you get the point—and taking them to Shady Pines 2.0, which, like a phoenix, arose from the ashes of the old Shady Pines. That baker was Sophia Petrillo, and those cheesecakes became legend.

Sophia bakes and bakes, memories of the Daughters of Sicily cook-off victory spurring her on to ever greater cheesecake masterpieces. Her near-tropical locale brings inspiration—coconut cheesecake topped with a pineappley glaze, for example, or the sunny flavor of lemon infused into cheesecake cupcakes. But mostly she relies on tried-and-true family recipes with a definite Italian flair, like a cheesecake that melds all the flavors of cannoli filling into a not-too-sweet homage to Sophia's favorite Brooklyn bakery. Of course, there's also the treasured Petrillo family recipe for Double Fudge Amaretto Ricotta Cheesecake. Given the fact that her great-great grandchildren sometimes stop by to lend a hand with the cheesecake prep, the recipes in Sophia's repertoire have every chance of sticking around for another hundred years.

Double Fudge Amaretto Ricotta Cheesecake

MAKES 16 SERVINGS

A Petrillo family secret—until now—this cheesecake manages to be rich and not too heavy at the same time. Thank you, ricotta. A splash of amaretto soaks in while the cheesecake cools. If the amaretti cookies are gluten-free, the whole cake will be, too.

Softened butter for the cake pan

6 ounces bittersweet chocolate (70%), coarsely broken or chopped

⅔ cup heavy cream

1 pound cream cheese, at room temperature

¾ cup sugar

¼ cup unsweetened cocoa

2 tablespoons cornstarch

½ teaspoon salt

4 large eggs, at room temperature

One 15-ounce container whole-milk ricotta (see note)

2 tablespoons amaretto or other almond liqueur

FOR THE TOPPING:

1 cup mascarpone cheese

2 tablespoons sugar

Large pinch salt

6 to 12 (depending on size) coarsely crumbled regular or gluten-free amaretti cookies

Heat the oven to 325°F with a rack in the center position. Butter the sides and bottom of a 9-inch springform pan. Prepare the pan for a water bath as described on page 38 and put it in a roasting pan. Keep a kettle of water hot over low heat.

Heat the chocolate and heavy cream in a small saucepan over very low heat, whisking occasionally, until the chocolate is completely melted and the mixture is smooth and shiny. Remove from the heat and keep the mixture in the warm saucepan while making the batter.

Using a handheld mixer or stand mixer with the paddle attachment, beat the cream cheese, sugar, cocoa, cornstarch, and salt together on medium-low speed just until creamy and lump-free, stopping to scrape down the bowl a few times. Add the eggs one at a time, mixing at low speed, waiting for each to be blended in before adding another. Stop once or twice to scrape down the bowl. Whisk in the chocolate mixture and then the ricotta by hand until thoroughly blended. Give the batter one last big stir and scrape it into the prepared pan.

Pull out the oven rack, put the roasting pan on the rack, and pour in enough hot water to reach about 1 inch up the sides of the cake pan. Carefully slide the rack back in. Immediately lower the oven temperature to 275°F. Bake until most of the cake is set and just the very center is a little jiggly, about 1½ hours. (Don't check until at least 1 hour and 15 minutes into the baking.) Turn off the oven and leave the door slightly ajar. Cool the cake in the oven until the oven is completely cool, about an hour. Move the cake from

(continued on page 134)

(continued from page 132)

the roasting pan to a cooling rack. Pour the amaretto over the top. Cool the cake to room temperature while it soaks up the amaretto. Remove the sides of the pan. Chill at least 6 hours and preferably overnight.

Just before serving, stir the mascarpone, 2 tablespoons sugar, and pinch of salt together just until blended—don't overmix. (See Golden Wisdom on page 146). Swirl the topping over the chilled cake, leaving a half inch or so border around the edges. Scatter the crumbled amaretti over the topping. Cut and serve according to the Tips on page 36.

Note: There are all kinds of ricotta available out there. For this cake, choose a whole-milk supermarket brand. Freshly made ricotta may be too wet.

DOROTHY: *What are you cooking now, Ma?*

SOPHIA: *A Petrillo family delicacy. Double fudge amaretto ricotta cheesecake.*

ROSE: *What's in it?*

Neapolitan Ice Cream Cheesecake

MAKES 16 SERVINGS

Too bad the Daughters of Sicily cook-off didn't have a dessert category; Louise Pallito wouldn't have stood a chance against this Tour de France! The cake requires several steps to put together, but because it must be done ahead, it's the perfect dessert for a big do. Sophia could even serve it for her own wake and still have plenty of time to get dressed (corsage and all).

4 ounces semisweet (62% or so) chocolate

Softened butter for the pans

1 Straight Outta Brooklyn Creamy Cheesecake (page 50), minus the crust

1 quart strawberry ice cream

Ganache (page 27), optional

Heat oven to 325°F with a rack in the center position. Butter two 9-inch round cake pans (regular cake pans, not springform) and line with parchment paper circles. Melt the chocolate in a double boiler and keep warm (see Golden Wisdom following the recipe for Double Fudge Chocolate Cheesecake on page 52).

Make the batter for Dorothy's Straight Outta Brooklyn Creamy Cheesecake. Pour half the batter (about 3 cups) into one of the prepared pans. Scrape the melted chocolate into the remaining half of the batter and stir until completely blended. Scrape the chocolate batter into the second pan. Bake side by side without a water bath until about 2 inches around the edges of the cakes are firm and the centers are slightly jiggly, about 25 minutes. It's likely that the chocolate cheesecake will take 5 minutes or so longer to cook. Turn off the oven and leave the door slightly ajar. Cool the cakes in the oven until the oven is completely cool, about an hour. Move the cakes from the oven to a cooling rack and cool to room temperature. Remove the cakes from the pans by placing a large flat plate over the pan and flipping the cake pan over. If necessary, tap lightly on the bottom of the pan to release the cake. If the edges of the cakes rose and are a little higher than the center, trim the sides even with the center for a nicer presentation. Wrap the layers individually in plastic wrap. The cake layers can be made up to two days in advance.

One day before serving, remove the strawberry ice cream to the refrigerator until softened enough to spread, about 1 hour. Check

(continued on next page)

(continued from previous page)

every 10 minutes or so after half an hour. Unwrap the chocolate layer and place in a 9-inch springform pan, flat side down. Spread the softened ice cream evenly over the chocolate layer. (Work quickly; you'll have a chance to clean it up later.) Top with the other layer, flat side up, pressing very gently to even out the ice cream. Close up the springform pan and put the cake in the freezer. Let freeze at least 4 hours and up to overnight.

Once the cake is frozen and the ice cream is firm again, remove the sides of the pan. Clean up the edges by scraping them with the back of a knife. To make a really sharp presentation, trim the sides of the cake with a knife to make them perfectly straight and smooth. Wrap the cake with plastic wrap and return to the freezer.

About 40 minutes to an hour before serving, unwrap the cake and put it on a serving plate or cake stand. Move it to the refrigerator. If serving the cake with ganache, make the ganache while the cake is softening in the refrigerator. The cake is ready to top with ganache, if using, and to serve when a paring knife meets little resistance when poked into the cake in a few places.

To top the cake with ganache, pour the finished ganache over the center of the cake and let it run over the cake and down the sides. Cut the cake and serve. Keep any leftover cake in the freezer and soften in the refrigerator again before serving.

MAX WEINSTOCK: *Sophia, I think we got a problem here.*

ROSE: *Is there anything we can do, Sophia?*

SOPHIA: *Go get two cheesecakes and wait up for me. I have a feeling the four of us will be talking till dawn.*

Cannoli Cheesecake

MAKES 16 SERVINGS

Everything you love about cannoli, but in a cheesecake: creamy ricotta, chocolate chips, a touch of orange marmalade, and a hint of cinnamon.

Baked Sugar Cookie Crust (page 22)

Softened butter for the pan

One 10-ounce package mini chocolate chips

1 teaspoon flour

¾ cup sugar

4 teaspoons cornstarch

½ teaspoon ground cinnamon

3 large eggs plus 1 yolk, at room temperature

1½ teaspoons vanilla extract

⅓ cup orange marmalade

Two 15-ounce containers whole-milk ricotta

Heat the oven to 350°F with a rack in the center position. Butter the sides of the springform pan. Prepare the pan for a water bath as described on page 38 and put it in a roasting pan. Keep a kettle of water hot over low heat.

Toss 1 cup of the chocolate chips and the flour together in a small bowl until the chips are coated. Set aside the bowl and the rest of the (unfloured) chips. Stir the sugar, cornstarch, and cinnamon together in a large bowl. Add the eggs, yolk, and vanilla and beat until foamy and blended. Scrape down the bowl and beat in the marmalade. Switch to a rubber spatula and beat in the ricotta. Save a few tablespoons of the coated chips and stir the rest into the batter.

Scrape the batter into the pan and gently wiggle to even out the top. Sprinkle the reserved coated chips over the top of the batter. Pull out the oven rack, put the roasting pan on the rack, and pour in enough hot water to reach about 1 inch up the sides of the cake pan. Carefully slide the rack back in. Immediately lower the oven temperature to 300°F. Bake until about 3 inches around the edges of the cake are firm and the center is slightly jiggly, about 1 hour to 1 hour and 10 minutes. (Don't check until at least 45 minutes into the baking.) Turn off the oven and leave the door slightly ajar. Cool, chill, and serve according to the Tips on page 36.

Options:

* Pipe rosettes of unsweetened whipped cream all around the edges of the chilled cake.

* Top the rosettes with coarsely chopped pistachios.

* Or just scatter the chopped pistachios over the cake.

* If you live near a bakery that fills its own cannoli, ask to buy a couple of the empty shells. Use a rolling pin to crush them into fine crumbs, then make a ring of crushed cannoli shells around the outer border of the top of the chilled cake.

Piña Colada Cheesecake

MAKES 16 SERVINGS

Maybe Dorothy, Blanche, and Rose should have opted out of their "luxury" vacation and stayed home to enjoy one of Sophia's Piña Colada cheesecakes instead. They would have gotten that tropical vibe without a militant bellhop and the sharing-a-bathroom-with-three-men thing. This creamy, coconutty cake with its pineapple topping that's to die for is perfect for the next time you fire up the tiki torches and bring the grass skirt out of mothballs. Got those little paper umbrellas that sometimes adorn Polynesian-style drinks? Open a few and put them in the center of the cake. If you're going to kitsch out, may as well go all the way.

1½ pounds cream cheese, at room temperature

½ cup sugar

4 teaspoons cornstarch

½ teaspoon salt

3 large eggs, at room temperature

⅔ cup canned cream of coconut

½ cup sour cream

2 tablespoons light rum or 1½ teaspoons vanilla extract

FOR THE PINEAPPLE TOPPING:
See page 29

Heat the oven to 350°F with a rack in the center position. Butter the springform pan and line it with parchment paper. Prepare the pan for a water bath as described on page 38 and put it in a roasting pan. Keep a kettle of water hot over low heat.

Using a handheld mixer or stand mixer with the paddle attachment, beat the cream cheese, sugar, cornstarch, and salt together on medium-low speed just until creamy and lump-free, stopping a few times to scrape down the bowl. Beat in the eggs one by one, scraping down the bowl about halfway through. Switch to low speed and stir in the cream of coconut, sour cream, and rum or vanilla.

Scrape the batter into the pan and gently wiggle to even out the top. Pull out the oven rack, put the roasting pan on the rack, and pour in enough hot water to reach about 1 inch up the sides of the cake pan. Carefully slide the rack back in. Immediately lower the oven temperature to 300°F. Bake until about 2 inches around the edges of the cake are firm and the center is slightly jiggly, 60 to 65 minutes. (Don't check until at least 50 minutes into the baking.) Turn off the oven and leave the door slightly ajar. Cool and chill the cake according to the Tips on page 36.

Up to four hours before serving the cake, make the topping. When the topping is completely cool, spoon room-temperature topping over slices of cheesecake when serving, or spread the cooled topping on the entire chilled cheesecake and refrigerate at least 30 minutes and up to several hours.

Option: Make the Vanilla Wafer Crust (page 20) and use it to line the bottom and sides of the pan, then bake.

Golden Wisdom: If you need just a little bit of a specialty liqueur like pineapple vodka but don't want to commit to a whole bottle, search the assortment of "airplane bottles" at your favorite liquor store. You'll be surprised at the variety a well-stocked store will carry.

RICK (fellow vacationer): *So, how have you ladies been enjoying your vacation?*

DOROTHY: *As a child during the Depression, I had to have my wisdom teeth extracted by a shoemaker. That was more fun than this.*

Limoncello Cheesecake Cupcakes

MAKES 12 CUPCAKES

Picture it: Sicily, the day before yesterday. Somebody somewhere is making limoncello. If there isn't a limoncello maker in your neighborhood, spring for a bottle and keep it on hand for an after-dinner drink or to drizzle over vanilla ice cream (with a smaller drizzle of olive oil!). Think of these as portable personal cheesecakes.

Nonstick cooking spray

1 pound cream cheese, at room temperature

½ cup sugar

2 teaspoons cornstarch

¼ teaspoon salt

1 large egg plus 1 yolk, at room temperature

½ cup heavy cream

3 tablespoons limoncello

Grated zest and juice of 1 lemon

Golden Wisdom: Use sturdy cupcake liners, especially if you plan to serve these right in the cup. There are a lot of choices out there, including foil cups already inside a separate paper cup. Many of this type have very festive outer papers—perfect! If you are using regular cupcake liners, simply double them up.

Line the compartments of a 12-cup regular (not jumbo) muffin tin with standard-size (about 2 inches deep and wide) paper cupcake liners. Spray the liners lightly with nonstick cooking spray. Heat the oven to 325°F with a rack in the center position.

Using a handheld mixer or stand mixer with the paddle attachment, beat the cream cheese, sugar, cornstarch, and salt together at medium speed just until creamy and lump-free, stopping once or twice to scrape down the bowl. Beat in the egg and yolk and scrape the bowl again. Use the rubber spatula to stir in the heavy cream, limoncello, lemon juice, and zest by hand, scraping the bowl once or twice as you mix.

Spoon the batter into the cups, dividing it evenly. Bake 10 minutes. Rotate the muffin tin front to back and continue baking until the cupcakes are jiggly just in the very center, 5 to 10 minutes more. Turn off the oven, open the door completely, and leave the cupcakes inside until the oven is cool, about 15 minutes. (The centers of the cupcakes will fall slightly as they cool.) Chill right in the tray at least 4 hours and up to overnight before serving. Sift confectioners' sugar over the tops immediately before serving. Serve right out of the cupcake liners or peel off the papers and line the cupcakes up on a serving platter.

Options:
* Put a mini vanilla wafer into the bottom of each cup before scraping in the batter and put another on top before baking.

* Spoon a small dollop of Crushed Raspberry Whipped Cream (page 28) onto the top of each cupcake.

* Dollop a little lemon topping onto each. Whip ½ cup chilled heavy cream and 1 tablespoon confectioners' sugar in a chilled bowl until it holds soft peaks. Spoon a small dollop of whipped cream onto each cupcake and pinch a little lemon zest over the cream, then plunk a mini vanilla wafer into the lemon topping if you like.

Zabaglione-Berry Cheesecake

MAKES 16 SERVINGS

Zabaglione is tough to pronounce even if your dentures aren't slipping. The classic ingredients that Sophia put into the zabaglione she baked for "Father" Angelo—marsala, eggs, and sugar—yield a cheesecake that is a perfect match for berries. In this case, the berries are both fresh and in the form of preserves. Mascarpone adds richness, and the juicy berries add a sweet-tart oomph. The swirls of raspberry preserves are flat-out fun and delicious.

Softened butter for the pan

1 pound cream cheese, at room temperature

1 cup granulated sugar

2 tablespoons cornstarch

½ teaspoon salt

4 large eggs, at room temperature

1 cup mascarpone, at room temperature

⅓ cup sweet marsala

1½ teaspoons vanilla extract

½ cup raspberry jam

FOR THE BERRY TOPPING:

3 cups mixed berries (a combo of raspberries, blackberries, and blueberries is nice)

2 to 3 tablespoons sugar

Half a lemon (on standby)

Heat the oven to 350°F with a rack in the center position. Butter a 9-inch springform pan and line the bottom with a parchment circle. Prepare the pan for a water bath as described on page 38 and put it in a roasting pan. Keep a kettle of water hot over low heat.

Using a handheld mixer or stand mixer with the paddle attachment, beat the cream cheese, sugar, cornstarch, and salt together on medium-low speed just until creamy and lump-free, stopping a few times to scrape down the bowl. Beat in the eggs, adding them quickly one after another and stopping about halfway through to scrape down the bowl. Switch to a whisk and beat in the mascarpone, marsala, and vanilla by hand. (See Golden Wisdom on the next page.) Scrape the bowl well to make sure there are no lumps and the batter is well mixed. Pour the batter into the pan. Spoon small dollops of preserves over the batter, dotting them more or less evenly across the top. Using a butter knife, gently swirl the preserves into the batter, making sure not to poke through the crust (if using). Swirl just enough to make big streaks of jam throughout the batter—don't overfold! Gently wiggle the pan to even out the top.

Pull out the oven rack, put the roasting pan on the rack, and pour in enough hot water to reach about 1 inch up the sides of the cake pan. Carefully slide the rack back in. Immediately lower the oven temperature to 300°F. Bake until about 3 inches around the edges of the cake are firm and the center is slightly jiggly, about 1½ hours. (Don't check until at least 1 hour into the baking.) Turn off

(continued on next page)

(continued from previous page)

the oven and leave the door slightly ajar. Cool and chill according to the directions on page 36.

30 minutes to an hour before serving, toss the berries with 2 tablespoons sugar. Let them stand, tossing gently once or twice. Taste and add up to another tablespoon of sugar and/or a squirt of lemon juice if the berries need it. Top each slice of cheesecake with a generous spoonful of berries. Resist the urge to top the whole cake with the berries unless you plan to serve the entire thing at once; the berries will make the top of the cake soggy if left too long.

Golden Wisdom: Mascarpone will curdle and separate like overwhipped heavy cream if beaten too long, so it is added at the very end of mixing the batter. Remember this when making other dishes with mascarpone, such as tiramisu.

Option: Make the Vanilla Wafer Crust or Graham Cracker crust and use it to line the bottom and sides of the pan (see page 15), using a parchment circle if you like. Bake the crust 10 minutes and cool while making the batter.

The Golden Girls Cookbook

Italian Coffee Cocktail

MAKES 2 DRINKS

A little coffee, a little anisette—they make a welcome finish to any Italian meal. Why wait until the end of the meal? Start off your evening with the same combo, only in an icy, well-shaken version. Don't forget the lemon twists!

¼ cup strong espresso or *very* strong brewed coffee, cooled to room temperature

2 ounces coffee liqueur

2 ounces anisette liqueur

2 lemon twists

Fill a large cocktail shaker with ice. Pour in the espresso and liqueurs. Shake vigorously and strain into 2 coupes or small martini glasses. Garnish with the lemon twists.

Option: For a frozen variation, put the espresso and liqueurs into a blender. Add 1½ cups crushed ice. Blend on low speed until the ice is fairly well crushed. Increase the speed to medium and blend until the ice is as smooth or chunky as you like. Pour into tall glasses or frozen coffee mugs.

Harvey Wallbanger

MAKES 1 DRINK

Picture it: Brooklyn, 1968. The Petrillo family lives up the block from a guy by the name of Harvey Wallbanger. (Don't ask!) One day, he walks into Sal and Sophia's apartment with a bottle of Galliano as a gift. Sophia has some OJ in the fridge; Sal digs a bottle of vodka out from his shaving kit ("Where the hell did that come from?" Sophia asks). This recipe originated with and is dependent on Galliano; however, versions made with anisette or even ouzo would be nice. This super-simple beverage is great for a cocktail-driven brunch. For a nicer presentation, drop several orange half-slices into a glass carafe and pour the liquor of choice over them a few hours before serving.

1½ ounces (3 tablespoons) vodka

3 ounces (generous ⅓ cup) orange juice

¾ ounce (1½ tablespoons) Galliano

Orange cubes (page 44) and/or maraschino cherries for garnish, optional

Fill a tall glass with ice and pour the vodka and orange juice over the ice. Stir well. Float the Galliano over the drink by pouring it slowly over the back of the spoon. Garnish with loose or skewered oranges and/or cherries if you like.

Option: Make a Dimitrios Wallbanger by substituting ouzo, a Greek spirit with a pronounced anise flavor, for the Galliano.

SOPHIA: *Remember what your cousin Frederico used to say: "People waste their time pondering whether a glass is half empty or half full. Me, I just drink whatever's in the glass."*

Raspberry Fizzle

MAKES ABOUT 4 FIZZLES

There are other things you can add to champagne besides salt. They may not get you out of paying the dinner tab, but they taste much, much better. One simple way to an elegant drink is a drizzle of raspberry puree and the addition of a fresh raspberry or two. Sub ginger ale (regular or diet) or sparkling cider for the champagne and you've got an alcohol-free version that is just as elegant.

1 orange, optional

4 sugar cubes

Slightly sweet sparkling wine, such as Asti; ginger ale; or sparkling cider

A drizzle (about 2 teaspoons) per glass Raspberry Sauce for Drizzling (page 28)

Fresh raspberries (extra points for golden raspberries), optional

If using the orange, rub the sugar cubes over the zest until they pick up color and have that wonderful fresh-orange smell. Drop a cube into each glass. Drizzle the raspberry puree over the sugar. Slowly pour in enough of the sparkling wine, ginger ale, or sparkling cider to fill the glass about two-thirds full. Slip in the berries, if using, and let them bob around in the bubbles.

SOPHIA: *If this sauce was a person, I would get naked and make love to it.*

Negroni

MAKES 1 DRINK

So you're relaxing on the lanai, getting ready to grill a little dinner. Suddenly a man in a crow costume parachutes down from the sky onto the lanai. Do you panic? No, you walk directly to the cabinet where you store the booze, mix up a negroni, and march back out to the lanai. Problem solved.

1 ounce (2 tablespoons) gin

1 ounce (2 tablespoons) sweet red vermouth

1 ounce (2 tablespoons) Italian red bitter, preferably (and classically) Campari

Orange twist for garnish, optional

Fill a rocks or Old Fashioned glass with ice, preferably cracked. (This drink works nicely in a tall thin glass as well.) Pour the gin, vermouth, and bitter over the ice. Stir well, slip in an orange twist, if you like, and serve.

> **BLANCHE:** *Well, I certainly didn't wait for my wedding night, honey. I couldn't. I had these urges. You know, in the South, we mature faster. I think it's the heat.*
>
> **DOROTHY:** *I think it's the gin.*

The Salty Chihuahua

MAKES 1 CHIHUAHUA

Sophia is a little like a Chihuahua: tiny with a big bark, which is usually on par with her bite. The Salty Chihuahua, a tequila-based take on the traditional Salty Dog, has both bark *and* bite. And that suits Sophia just fine.

Kosher or coarse sea salt

Lime wedge

1½ ounces (3 tablespoons) tequila

½ ounce (1 tablespoon) orange liqueur

4 ounces (½ cup) pink grapefruit juice

Spread out the salt on a plate. Rub the rim of a tall glass with the lime wedge, then dip the glass into the salt. Pour the tequila and orange liqueur into the glass and add enough ice to fill the glass two-thirds full. Pour in the grapefruit juice, give the drink a little stir, and garnish with the lime wedge.

Option: Serve the Salty Chihuahua shaken and up: Salt the rim of a coupe or small martini glass as described above. Fill a cocktail shaker two-thirds full of ice. Pour the tequila, orange liqueur, and grapefruit juice over the ice. Cover the shaker and shake well. Strain into the salted glass and garnish with the lime wedge.

DOROTHY: *Ma, what is that you're knitting?*

SOPHIA: *A bottle cover for the sherry.*

DOROTHY: *Why do we need to cover the sherry?*

SOPHIA: *Not the sherry here in the house. The sherry I take to the park. You drink out of a paper bag in the park and suddenly everybody's your friend.*

ROSE: *Oh, Sophia, I don't think it's a good idea to drink in the park.*

SOPHIA: *Hey, I do it once a month with the girls from the Cloud Society.*

BLANCHE: *The Cloud Society?*

SOPHIA: *Yeah, we stake out a bench, knock a few sherries back, and discuss what we think the clouds look like. One afternoon, I thought I saw Pat Sajak riding sidesaddle on a dolphin.*

SOPHIA'S GUIDE TO CAFFÈ CORRETTO

Caffè corretto, literally "corrected coffee," is a part of everyday life in all parts of Italy. Visit any Italian "bar" on any given morning and you'll see quite a few of these being prepared. In rural parts of the country, you'll see farmers and grocers taking part in this custom; in urban areas, people in business attire stop by on their way to the office. But caffè corretto can (and should!) be enjoyed any time of day, especially after a meal. The bartender makes an espresso, screws off the top of the requested correction, and adds a tiny shot—maybe a teaspoon. Caffè corretto works better than any alarm to give a jolt to your morning or snap you out of a midafternoon daze. The tiny amount of booze isn't meant for a buzz but rather a bracing backup to the caffeine kick. Here are a few ideas for corrections to enjoy any time of day. Let's borrow a page from Sophia's playbook and put this as bluntly as possible: the spirits used for a corretto don't need to be top shelf, but they should still be good quality.

CORRETTO ALLA GRAPPA

Grappa connoisseurs spend up to hundreds of dollars per bottle for rare or very special bottles. That kind of grappa isn't for a corretto. A reasonably priced grappa, not the cheapest you can find but a few steps up in price, is what you're looking for here.

CORRETTO ALLA BRANDY

"Brandy" is a pretty vague term. Choose a bottle of lower-priced French brandy or even one from California. Brandy mellows the coffee and adds a woody note to the corretto.

CORRETTO ALLA SAMBUCA

In addition to a little kick and wonderful anisey flavor, sambuca adds a little sweetness and makes the perfect finish to a meal.

CORRETTO ALL'AMARO

Italians often finish off a meal by sipping an *amaro* literally "bitter": a reference to the bitter, herbaceous flavor of these drinks. Correcting a coffee with amaro may not be to everyone's taste, but it is worth a shot, or half a shot in this case.

Golden Wisdom: No fancy espresso machine at home? Consider the moka pot, a small pot that sits atop a stove burner and brews espresso-strong coffee that is perfect for a corretto. Mokas have been and are a favorite in Italian (and Italian American) homes.